Up, Up and Away

Up, Up and Away

The Biography of BE FAIR

Lucinda Prior-Palmer

PELHAM BOOKS

First published in Great Britain by PELHAM BOOKS LTD
52 Bedford Square London WC1B 3EF
APRIL 1978
SECOND IMPRESSION BEFORE PUBLICATION

© Lucinda Prior-Palmer 1978 (By permission of the British Equestrian Federation, to whom a donation has been made)

All Rights Reserved. No part of this publication
may be recorded, stored in a retrieval system,
or transmitted, in any form or by any means,
electronic, mechanical, photocopying, recording
or otherwise, without the prior permission
of the Copyright owner

ISBN 0 7207 1041 3

Printed in Great Britain by
Hollen Street Press Ltd at Slough, Berkshire
and bound by Dorstel Press at Harlow Essex

To Daddy

Contents

	Acknowledgments	8
	Preface	9
1	A Horse of That Colour	11
2	The Alphabet	29
3	Learning, Learning	46
4	Out of the Nursery	70
5	Kick on	82
6	A Shaft of Light	105
7	Ups . . .	119
8	. . . and Downs	132
9	Trials and Errors	152
10	Some Put Their Trust in Horses	174
11	'The Greatest'	184
12	Olympic Build-up	202
13	Real Life	214
	Epilogue	240

Acknowledgments

To Caroline Silver; Barbara Cooper; Valerie Russell; Michael Sissons; Eric Marriott; Lesley Gowers; Clare Nightingale; and my family: without their help and guidance I would not have had enough confidence or determination to either start or complete this book.

To Fleur Clissold who typed the manuscript; her patience and dedication were unfailing through hours of deciphering sheets of script.

To Clive Hiles who kindly allowed his photographs to be used free of charge.

To Rosalind and Joss Hanbury who enabled me to live undisturbed whilst I scribbled away in the peaceful magic of their home, 'Burley on The Hill'.

Special Acknowledgment

To all those kind and hard-working people who rarely receive personal acknowledgment but without whom there would be no competitions and no story of Be Fair. Fence judges, course-builders, car-park attendants, St John Ambulance and Red Cross, arena parties, scorers, secretaries and organisers, are but a few of those to whom I would like to extend my warmest thanks.

Preface

This book is not written to display any particular literary skill but simply to tell the story of an exceptional horse, with whom I was lucky enough to form a special kind of partnership. I am told that such a relationship as this comes rarely more than once in a lifetime, be it with an animal or with a human.

As the story unfolded I noticed a number of lessons entangled in the various twists and turns. They may or may not be of help. They are, after all, only one person's interpretation of circumstance.

1 A Horse of That Colour

'Do you think that maybe we ought to sell him?' I asked my mother. 'If I thought anyone would give as much as £400 for him, I'd sell him tomorrow,' she replied.

Her meaning was clear. We had marooned ourselves with a problem horse and we had little alternative but to battle on and try to find dry land. Be Fair, our six year old chestnut gelding, looked every inch a class horse. In 1968 £525 was very little for a near thoroughbred of 16.2 hh, bred as well as he was, but shortly after the cheque was signed, it seemed far too much. He was living up to the hot-blooded, awkward reputation of his colour.

During my last half-term holiday from school in the autumn of 1968, I had noticed an advertisement in the *Horse and Hound*. 'Fair and Square' was printed in bold type at the bottom of one page. It seemed that his sole progeny was for sale. He would automatically be a brilliant event horse I assumed, as I read through the advertisement. Fair and Square had won the Burghley Three Day Event in September that autumn.

The advertisement that started it all

By FAIR and SQUARE

The outstanding Event horse and recent winner of the Burghley Three-Day Event. Unique opportunity to buy this horse's sole progeny, BE FAIR, 5½ yr old Thoroughbred Chestnut 16 hands 1½in. Broken and schooled by internationally known Horsemaster. Excellent basic Dressage training and jumping. Snaffle-mouthed, good in stable and traffic. Purchased by owner when 4 yr old for Eventing and Hunting. Unfortunately has not grown into a horse up to the owner's weight for Hunting. This is the sole reason for sale. Fair and Square's sire was Brightworthy.

Hollinsworth, Rectory Farm House, Tibberton, nr. Droitwich, Worcs. Tel.: Spetchley 268.

11

I showed the advertisement to my mother after lunch and our imagination ran amok. We decided that it must be just the horse we wanted – but not for at least a year. My pony, Sea Sway, was 14.2 hh and I was fourteen. She would last me for another year. No more was said and later we went for a walk in the cold, dreary November afternoon.

Suddenly my mother stopped, turned to me and said, 'We've got to go and see that horse – I have a feeling about him.'

By 6.00 the next morning, we were driving through that hollow type of blackness that comes before dawn, rain lashing the windscreen as we headed for Birmingham. An hour after dawn, we branched off the M1 motorway and into a series of attractive rural lanes leading to our destination, Hagley Hall.

The massive Victorian house seemed quite empty. Ivy crept across the wide-paned windows and up the door frame. We left the car in the drive and wandered past the lonely house, on through the archway into what was presumably the stable-yard. It was cobbled at least but there were no horses and no sign of anything else.

Footsteps on our right indicated that human life did exist. A girl of about twenty approached and asked if we had come to see the horse. I stared through the open door from which she had emerged. Slowly my eyes adjusted to the darkness within and made out a horse's head in the shadows. I moved closer and saw distinctly a chestnut face looking over a bar. Down the centre of the face was a narrow white marking resembling an inverted question-mark.

The light flashed on, the horse turned from the bar and withdrew to the back of his small stable. He stood there, surveying us without undue interest. His old jute rugs were taken off to reveal a ribby body. His coat had been clipped which gave him a yellowy, pale chestnut appearance. He looked lean and without any extra muscle.

The girl led him out of his stable across the cobbles and under the arch for us to see him trot in-hand, up and down the driveway. We did not notice much because we were not too sure what we were meant to be noticing but as he trotted towards us, even we realised that his near fore-leg did not move in a straight line. It seemed to swing round to the outside every time he picked it up. We vaguely wondered why. When he came to a halt we studied the offending limb and soon discovered the reason. An evil-looking scar ran right the way round his heel from one side of the hoof to the other. On closer inspection we noticed a vertical cut through his coronet band and straight down the hoof to the shoe. The girl explained that the year before his foot had become entangled in some wire. He must have pulled back violently, for when they found him in the field they were not certain that the wound would ever knit together again. It did heal but enclosed some dirt at the same time. The hoof then had to be slit open by the vet to drain out the pus. We were assured that it had caused no further trouble since and that the horse was perfectly all right.

All the way to Birmingham to see a horse with three feet? My mother was not best pleased, but then she did recall that the owner had mentioned something about an injury on the telephone the previous evening. In any case, we thought we might as well see him ridden as we had bothered to come all that way.

We followed on foot as Be Fair trotted down the tarmac drive. The girl put him into a canter on the grass verge and a few strides later they jumped into the surrounding park over 3′ 6″ of chestnut railings. My mother and I looked at each other, impressed. We watched him circle the great oaks and elms that must, over hundreds of years, have witnessed many different horses pass beneath them.

My mother had not ridden much since hunting a small pack of hounds in India before the war. Nonetheless, buying this horse was her responsibility and she felt she had better ride him herself. After a while she stretched him out to gallop. He tried, but it was a scratchy short stride that he produced and my mother was not so impressed.

Then it was my turn. I could not wait. He looked enormous to me for I had never ridden anything bigger than my pony. What would it feel like up there? I was given a leg up and set off cautiously at a walk. Soon we trotted and then risked a canter around the park, pleasantly surprised at feeling quite safe and not really overhorsed. I wanted to feel how he jumped and looked round for some little fences. There were only the park railings and they were rather imposing for my initial attempt at jumping a full-grown horse.

There were no other fences. If I wanted to jump it was the park railings or nothing. I turned and cantered Be Fair towards them.

It was the look on my face, the unconscious broad smile that spread across it from cheek to cheek, as I felt the majestic power of his jump unfold beneath me, that made my mother decide, against her better judgement, to buy the horse.

I owe Australia a great deal. It was occupying my father on business during that time and my mother had to take the final decision on her own. My father had been in the Cavalry for thirty-five years, over a decade of them at a time when they oiled horses and not tanks. He had long since forgotten more than my mother and I knew about horses. The day he was first taken to the riding school to see the new acquisition, he muttered laughingly 'You might at least have bought a horse which started off with four feet.' Otherwise he liked it very much.

My mother had been definitely windy about that foot and had put her faith in the vet, Mr Cullen, who was asked to go and examine Be Fair at Hagley Hall and preferably to ride him too, in order to tell my mother whether or not he thought the horse a worthwhile purchase. It never occurred to her that maybe the vet did not know how to ride.

Fortunately he did, and when he telephoned that night to say he had passed the horse, he told my mother that he liked the ride it had given him. If it was the one he thought had been advertised in the *Horse and Hound,* then for £525 she was 'getting a bit of a bargain,' according to him.

The 7th of November, 1968 was my fifteenth birthday. I was back at school and, having heard nothing from home, had presumed, somewhat sadly, that my mother had refrained from buying Be Fair. A greetings telegram awaited me on the letter board. I ripped it open.

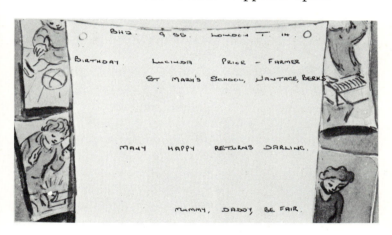

It took a few seconds to sink in. Be Fair was written so innocuously beside Mummy and Daddy. Slowly I absorbed the full meaning of the telegram. Be Fair was mine, my very own; I felt grown up at last – I had a real horse.

The following week a letter came from home, describing Be Fair's journey south. Mr Cook, who for nearly thirty years has been 'Mr Do Everything' at Appleshaw, our home in Hampshire, took the trailer up to Birmingham behind our very old, ex-air force Land Rover, named Sunshine. She was called that because of her bright yellow bonnet which used to warn aircraft not to land on her. Fortunately he took Mrs Cook with him because after only a quarter of their journey, the windscreen wipers broke and the sleet started to freeze onto the windscreen. Mrs Cook became the human spare set, disembarking every few miles to give another scratch with her frost-bitten fingers and another wipe with an oil-stained rag.

Cold and miserable, they arrived at Hagley five hours later. Two and a half hours later they left again. The goods had taken that long to load. I thought it was quite amusing when I first heard that Be Fair had refused every persuasion to enter the trailer for that length of time because Sea Sway had always needed lengthy encouragement to go into the trailer, as well.

But refusing to load was only the hors d'oeuvre to a banquet of very naughty tricks. By the time the next visiting week-end arrived I had already been notified by another letter that this new horse appeared to have quite a mind of his own. Life with him would not be all plain sailing.

I went home on Saturday and that afternoon I rode Be Fair out with Mrs Skelton who kept the local riding school where Be Fair was stabled and who had taught me to ride every Tuesday and Thursday since I was four. Sometimes she let me show or hunt one of her ponies.

The mixed feelings of excitement and pride in riding my very own proper horse for the first time were soon transformed into feelings of dismay. Balancing on his hind-legs, Be Fair whipped round twice on the road in the first half mile, showing the whites of his eyes as he 'spooked at' and refused to pass a leaf or a sweet-paper, until given a lead by the accompanying horse ridden by Mrs S.

Riding my very own 'proper' horse for the first time

My father wanted to see how our new horse jumped and we decided to pop him round Mrs Skelton's mini cross-country course that same afternoon. Without any problems we jumped the first fence twice to warm up before setting off round the course. That, however, was as far as we went. Be Fair flatly refused even to approach it a third time. Once again he stood on his hind-legs at well-timed and frequent intervals as he reversed across the field towards the gate that led homewards. There was nothing I could do but sit there; the more I kicked or turned or pulled, the faster he reversed and the higher he reared. He overdid it that day and fell over backwards. That was enough to knock co-operation into him for the afternoon's duration – but no longer. He never went over backwards again – he minded far too much about Number One to do that, but his napping and rearing and absolute refusal to co-operate if he did not feel like it, continued with resolve.

We did not know what to do with him. He had a mind of his own and he knew how to use it to his best advantage. Would there ever be a way of curing him of these beastly habits? I realised then what my mother had meant: no one would want to pay £400 for his bent ideas on how to be a lovely horse.

Later that year we sent him to Mrs Firth. She had sold us my second pony and she was the only adult we knew who rode well enough and, unlike Mrs S., had the time to try and sort out Be Fair.

She thought she would have the time. She had four children all under twelve and three hunters, but she had a girl groom and she thought she would have plenty of time to teach a young horse a few manners so that a teenager could enjoy riding him.

The washing piled up, the iron had a holiday. Letters lay about the house unanswered, some even went unopened. The family chose to eat out of tins in preference to staring at empty dishes. Be Fair was holding the Firth family to ransom. If they would not allow him his own life-style, then he certainly would not allow them theirs. They battled for hours in the stable-yard, in the field, on Salisbury Plain and on the roads. It soon became evident that it was necessary for Major Firth to follow Be Fair down the roads in his Land Rover with a long lunge whip protruding from the window. Every time Be Fair whipped round at a dustbin or a bicycle or some such obscure object from outer space, he would see the lunge whip. If he still refused to move in the required direction, he would come face to face with Major Firth in person, who, having climbed out of the Land Rover would advance towards him, whip in hand. Only then would he know he had lost and in general prefer to do as he was told, rather than have a sore bottom.

Occasionally during the holidays I was driven over to Urchfont to ride the 'town horse'. Mrs Firth nicknamed him this as he would not walk through puddles or over drainage ditches or do anything that a country child would be expected to do. Sometimes she called him the yellow horse but I preferred to call him red. He never was given a serious stable name as nothing seemed to suit him.

He learnt very quickly that my legs were neither as long nor as strong as Mrs Firth's and the Land Rover had to follow even closer when I rode him. Nor was he slow to realise that the Land Rover could not follow him across jumps. Whereas he would jump quite a big post and rails or a hedge without dispute, he stubbornly refused to take off over anything the least bit trappy or ditch-like no matter how minute. It was always a case of who became bored first as to who won. If you were prepared to try for long enough, sometimes for several hours, in the very end he would give in. This was no help in any small educational competitions that Mrs Firth wanted to take him to. The local riding club One Day Event at Wylye in Wiltshire produced the usual scenes of battle but he did in the end complete the cross-country course, because a horse would eventually overtake him at every fence he was arguing over, thus giving him a lead which he consented to follow.

During early spring my mother and I went to watch Be Fair's father, Fair and Square, compete at the Crookham Two Day Event. Firstly we watched some of the dressage tests. It was very complicated trying to follow the movements of the test printed in the programme as each horse performed them. There was something called 'on two tracks' which I gradually realised meant going sideways and not, as I had imagined, completing the movement twice in separate parallel lines. It was very exciting as Sheila Willcox, standing nearby on Fair and Square, talked to us for a little when my mother told her that we owned his sole progeny.

'You see that telegraph pole?' she asked us, pointing to a horizontal post. 'I know Fair and Square would jump it at exactly the point I asked him to. He is dead obedient and dead accurate; that is what makes him such a good horse.'

Encouraging words, as I knew I was lucky if Be Fair even took off over a fence, let alone jumped it at a predestined spot.

We endeavoured to dig up his shady past to see whether it would help us throw some light on the present problem. We discovered that a Miss Joan Rymer from Gloucestershire had owned a classically bred mare named Happy Reunion. The mare broke down hunting in her old age and several marriages for her were arranged but she was not interested. As a last resort the mare was left in a field with a two-year-old Brightworthy colt that Miss Rymer also owned.

Eleven months later Be Fair took his first look at the world he intended to take on.

Happy Reunion, Be Fair's apparently barren mother

Be Fair as an untidy two year old . . .

The youngster lived the preliminary three years of his life not far from the Gloucestershire seat of the Duke of Beaufort, lazing in pastures, well fed and rather fat. He was then sold to a Mr Spano and it was decided to begin his training and break him in. The gelding, however, had other ideas and Jekyll, the biddable three year old, transformed himself, with surprising alacrity, into Hyde whose motto was 'I shan't'. With a naturally strong will and an inventive mind, he quickly adopted a policy of

. . . but looking better as a three year old in 1966 (*Findlay Davidson*)

non-co-operation and would simply lie down at the end of the white lunge-rein whenever he was lunged in a circle. Two well-known establishments failed to find the solution for Mr Spano. David Tatlow, famous producer of show horses and champion point-to-point jockey, was the third to try. By realising that this was a horse that would never suffer domination, he decided to meet him halfway, and with the necessary patience and firmness he succeeded in keeping the three year old from turning his back to the blackboard and duly taught him to accept a bridle, a saddle and eventually a rider.

Mr Spano knew that he was dying. In the winter of 1967 he sent his newly broken four year old to be schooled at Lars Sederholm's Oxfordshire establishment so that he should be well sold afterwards.

The 1969 Badminton winner Richard Walker, who worked for many years under Lars, vaguely remembers Be Fair in those early days. Not very favourably however, for he spent many long hours battling with him over a tiny ditch and many other problems. He did remember

Be Fair at four years old – not the lovely horse he thought he was

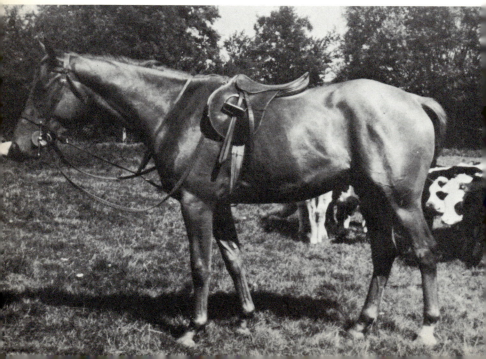

him as a nice type of horse though, but when Be Fair came up for sale they knew him too well and did not want to buy him.

He *was* a nice type of horse and a Birmingham businessman paid well for him as a four year old in 1967.

Two years later and after two months of spring grass with us at Appleshaw, Be Fair returned to the Firths to continue his next term at reform school. With him went two bottles of mysterious content and a box of powder. Once mixed together these ingredients formed a special 'set as you mix' cement, which we had been given to plaster up a gap in his hoof. A quarter of it had had to be cut away as more dirt had intruded and once again the foot was beginning to fester from the inside. The gap on the near-fore was further encouraged not to lever apart by a special shoe being fitted which had a toe-clip at either side of the crack. This design of shoe he wore all his life.

My legs were growing; I would soon need roller-skates if I was to continue riding Sea Sway. The transition to Be Fair must be made before we had to sell Sea Sway. It was clear that I was not going to be given a 15.2 hh kind and gentle stepping-stone but then I did not really want one. I wanted to learn to ride my proper horse as soon as possible.

At that time I was in fierce pursuit of a new saddle. Since I had started to ride I had used one of my father's pre-war polo saddles which used to grind against my backside so that sitting on it for more than half an hour became very painful.

St John Ambulance was holding a thirty-mile sponsored ride near Newbury. The prize for the most sponsorship money gained was a new saddle, made to measure by the Lambourn saddlers.

Not an especially ardent letter-writer, I nevertheless sat down and wrote to all my relations begging support for my backside. No distant aunt or twice-removed cousin were exempted from the plea, to which I added as an afterthought that their money would go to St John Ambulance, and one day they might need them too.

It was decided that I should take Be Fair and not Sea Sway, for if I rode him for thirty miles it would be a good opportunity for us to become a little more accustomed to one another.

We brought him home from Mrs Firth's the day before the sponsored ride and that evening my parents left aboard a boat bound for the Canary Islands and their holiday.

The next day Mr Cook and I, expecting the usual loading problems, left two hours in hand but still we arrived at our destination just in time. Shortly after we unloaded Be Fair, the first group set off on the start of their thirty mile ride and Be Fair thought he would like to go with them. He stood on his hind legs and shot round in ever decreasing circles as I tried to persuade him that his start time had not yet come. His neck darkened with sweat before we had even begun. None too soon I was started in a batch of about ten others, none of whom I knew. For a mile he pulled and yanked at my arms, convinced that if he did it with enough regularity and enough force they would drop off my body and he would be free to gallop away as fast as he could across the Berkshire Downs, thus beating everyone by at least twenty-eight miles.

After a fraction of the distance had been completed beneath the blazing hot September sun, the batch became strung out. Be Fair rightly concluded that it was not a race and settled down to enjoy the chalky contours of the countryside.

Some hours later we were on our own. About two miles back we had passed the final check-point and been told that we were well in time. Be Fair felt tired at which I was not surprised considering his behaviour at the beginning, but I felt sorry for him and climbed off and ran beside him for some of the way. The thought of the saddle spurred me to run further for I was nearly certain that I would win it. My sponsorship had totalled £43, and from what little I had overheard, that was more than the others had gathered.

Exhilaration flooded through me, I was no longer frightened of Be Fair, suddenly I felt 'as one' with him. My mother had often ridden him during that year and he had behaved as monstrously with her as he did with other people. Despite this she was convinced, because of the manner in which he misbehaved, that he was not evil, just very very naughty. As I climbed back on and trotted steadily along the top of a hill I too was convinced that this horse was genuinely not unkind. It was the first time since I had attempted to jump Mrs Skelton's mini cross-country course that I felt Be Fair might not be such a disaster after all. Perhaps trying to ride him was not going to prove quite such a lost cause as taking on my brother in a punch-up.

I came to the end of a track and looked for the arrows which had indicated the route so far. I could not see one so I turned in the direction which my nose presumed was correct and continued along the track. Two miles later it became clear that my nose had been wrong. The Downs were becoming wilder – civilisation and the finish must be receding. Be Fair was only too delighted to stand still for a few minutes while I looked out across miles of foreign territory and tried to find my bearings. Evening was drawing on, the air was cooler and fresher; only the song of an occasional bird broke the silence.

I was lost, unmistakably lost, and what was worse so was that saddle. I had no idea of which way to go and I knew that my time would soon expire. I felt hopeless and desperate and a lump welled up somewhere deep in the back of my parched throat. I dropped the reins on Be Fair's neck and told him that it was up to him to find the way back. I only hoped that his sense of direction was better than mine evidently was.

Be Fair trotted slowly and wearily back down the same track that we had just ventured up. I was forcibly reminded with every fall of my aching bottom of why I had ever started on the wretched ride in the first place. I saw visions of the beautiful new saddle. It was a revolting orangey colour and I was going to enjoy sousing it in a whole tin of darkening oil. Through long periods of guerilla warfare with my elder brother and his friends I had learnt not to cry, but this time the situation overcame my painful education.

An hour later a thin, weary chestnut horse plodded through the finish. Most of the other riders had either gone home or were loading prior to leaving. Mr Cook was still there looking bored and just a little vexed as he leant, hands in pockets, against Sunshine's yellow nose.

'Where've you been then?' he asked.

'I got lost,' I replied unnecessarily. The tears had dried and I hoped that no one would notice the clean channels they must have left down dusty cheeks. The organiser approached as I slid despondently and weakly to the ground.

'Awfully glad to see you,' she said, 'we were all a bit worried you'd never come back as we knew you didn't know the area. Apparently the teddy boys have been mucking about up on the Downs and pinched a few of the signs from up there; it's no wonder you got lost.'

That night my mother and father rang from the middle of the Bay of Biscay to enquire whether or not our first endurance test together had been a success. I told them that I had been lost for an hour but that Be Fair was wonderful. Tired as he was, he had brought me safely back and the organisers had decided to give us the voucher for the saddle, despite our having exceeded the time limit, since our £43 sponsorship was the highest achieved. I certainly did not admit to them that desperation had driven me to tears.

Be Fair's first hunter trial at the Hursley Pony Club

Before he returned to his school and I to mine, we decided to take Be Fair to a local Pony Club hunter trials to widen his horizons a little. The second fence was a narrow and insignificant natural ditch which ran across a flat field. Be Fair did nothing unusual. He stopped dead on the brink, reared up and whipped round to the right. I tried to pull him back left-handed and he continued to rear with his back to the ditch. This time, with the confidence gained the previous week, I reacted positively. Quickly I changed tactics and pulled right. As he reared

Competing with us in the pairs class is my pony Sea Sway with Lucilla Evers

he swung round, following my unexpected pull to the opposite side and once again faced the ditch. For a second he stood in front of it, making his decision: should he respond for me or should he continue with his familiar non-co-operation?

He made a decision then and he stuck to it for the rest of his life. Springing across the ditch, he progressed around the rest of the course without a flicker of hesitation and only a brief look at the following two ditches. Confirming his faith, that afternoon a schoolfriend, Lucilla Evers, rode Sea Sway in the pairs class with Be Fair and me. He marked his signing of the Magna Carta with a red rosette, a colour that neither of us were to see again for over two years.

Magna Carta signed, Be Fair collects his rosette

2 *The Alphabet*

Sea Sway had to be sold. She had been a very inexpensive purchase from Ireland and now, eighteen months later, she was a good reliable Pony Club mount and we had to pay for Be Fair. She fetched a good price and went to an especially kind home in Norfolk, and then our attention turned solely to Be Fair. If he did not work out, then there was nothing for it but the typewriter and the ghastly cocktail parties in London. I hoped that it would work out; I did not relish the prospect of the alternative.

We knew it was vital that he should hunt that winter, preferably with a pack of hounds across a good country scattered with every type of fence. He had to learn not to question his rider, he had to learn the meaning of the old phrase 'to go forwards of his own free will'. We were not sure where to send him. The hunting near us was inclined to be of the type which encouraged ladies to go out with their sandwiches and ginger-nuts. No one jumped much. Occasionally a Forestry Commission gate crossed one of the identical, endless, over-grown woodland rides. Shrieks of horror would be heard as ginger-nuts flew from hands eager to pull their horses up sharp and dive off the main track and down a side one. Of the few that boldly remained in canter it was foreseeable that the Forestry Commission might have one more repair job on their hands.

Friends suggested a certain farmer in the Pytchley country named Tom Payne. They assured us he had spent a lifetime with horses of every type and temperament and was one of Nature's gifts to a young horse.

In mid-November Be Fair found himself once again in the Midlands, this time nearer to Northampton than

Birmingham. Tom was a bit worried when he saw Be Fair for the first time. 'He already looks thin enough for it to be the back end of the season,' he said, 'and he's so small – 16.2 hh he might measure, but he doesn't look it; it must be his high-boned wither. But he's a small one really, and I've got very long legs, you know.'

He rode the young horse about his farm for a couple of days. He had nothing to jump nearby except a heap of bushes forming a prospective bonfire at the edge of a ploughed field. Be Fair jumped those all right so he decided to take him out hunting the next day.

Be Fair had apparently 'seen' hounds two winters before when he was at Hagley Hall but he had never hunted. He trembled with excitement as he joined the back of the field when they drew away from the meet towards the first covert. He wore a double-bridle but as Tom said, this was not to be used as air-brakes but simply so that he would not have to pull at the horse all the time. Tom always hunted a horse in a double and they always went well for him, but his touch was sensitive and his hands were exceptional.

Be Fair shook violently as he stood transfixed by the occasional hollow bay and the rustling of undergrowth that echoed from within the wood as hounds drew the covert. The sweat formed white foam down either side of his neck.

Without any warning the fox broke cover directly in front of him and ran between his legs swiftly followed by the hounds. Be Fair's trembling stopped. He was fossilised. The huntsman galloped past him blowing his horn. Be Fair remained rooted to the ground, every muscle in his body taut to breaking point. Tom's instinct told him to let the horse go; he sensed he might confirm this young horse's non-co-operation for life if he were to hold him back at that point. His common sense told him that as he had no idea if the horse could even jump properly, he was mad to let him go and he ought to stay at the back of the field which is the rightful place for a green young horse. Instinct won and Be Fair found himself alone with the huntsman; the hounds were in full cry across big Pytchley country and Be Fair kept pace with the wise hunter as they leapt from field to field.

Tom loves to recall the moment he realised just what calibre of horse he was riding:

'There was a sod of a fence down in the bottom corner of a field, a great hedge with a rail through it on to a messy bank and a socking great ditch the other side. No place to jump a novice, that I did know. But there was no option. I knew Be Fair must not be held back at any cost and so I let him follow the huntsman over this big trappy fence. Then, my God, if hounds didn't do an about turn and we had to jump back over this ruddy great thing with the ditch towards us this time. The little 'oss managed it and then I knew I was sittin' on something special. Be he a young 'un or not, he had courage.'

During that day the cement fell out of the hole in Be Fair's hoof. Tom never dared fill it up again because he was worried that he would block in some dirt. He left it well alone and it was never any more trouble for the rest of the horse's life.

During the Christmas holidays it was organised that I should have a day's hunting with the Pytchley on my own horse.

Firstly we had to overcome the obstacle of growing-up. Apparently I could not hunt a 16.2 hh horse with a smart pack of hounds in my tweed jacket, jodhpurs and short brown jodhpur boots. The moth balls were brushed off my mother's 1936 navy-blue hunting coat but the stringent odour stayed with it for at least half the day's hunting. White hunting ties and pins were unearthed from the depths of one of my father's drawers. A pair of black leather riding boots were purchased from an 'old world' London boot maker, where they were found to fit my leg better than the one they had been originally designed for. My father discovered his sets of highly polished spurs from cavalry days and bent one pair in so that it was a small enough arch to fit round the heel of my new boot. With this attire thrown into a gruesomely heavy canvas bag I trudged across London on the Underground to catch the appropriate train to the Midlands.

We were quite certain that I would fall off at the first possible opportunity just because I was wearing these smart semi-new clothes for the first time.

I did not fall off and after the early hoof-fulls of Pytchley clay were thrown up and caught me across the chest, back and legs, I felt happier and more relaxed. Be Fair behaved beautifully, he was well mannered and thoroughly in command of himself. Tom had persuaded him that life was really more pleasant for horses who co-operate and the ride he gave me was that of a lady's hunter. What a change.

There was no scent that day and we did not have much of a chance to jump which irritated me as I badly wanted to know how he fared over these big fences. The field were starting to look at their watches and swig the last of their brandy down into the depths of their chilled bodies, when suddenly the sound we had waited for all day burst upon the still of the countryside. It hung in an echo on the cold evening air. Hounds were in full cry and doubling back the way we had come. How lucky, I thought. I knew that there were three lovely wire-free hedges across the next two fields. I had regarded them with envy as we trotted through the gateways shortly before. At last we were going to be able to jump.

The field spread out and took the fences where they pleased. The fourth fence was a vast boundary hedge with a gaping ditch on the far side, giving on to a track. The field did not consist of timid old ladies, but they knew, one discovered later, that fence to be one of the few they never jumped; instead they galloped towards the gate in the corner. Be Fair and I cantered in all innocence across the field, then suddenly began to realise that no one was going to jump the large hedge in front of us. The steaming throng of some forty horses already piling up in the corner of the field resembled a mass of dirty, cooked, red and black currants, forcing their way through a conical strainer. My blood was up; I had been waiting all day to jump and now that we had started I could not bear to stop. By then we were only seven or eight strides from the boundary hedge and cantering slowly. Suddenly Be Fair felt a signal; he knew what Tom's legs meant, they meant go – fun coming, and he responded to mine in the same way. Three strides short of the hedge I saw through a thinning in it that we were going to land on a wooden stake, used to support the wire placed in front of the ditch when cattle were in the field. I pulled right as Be Fair launched into the air. He angled across the top of that gigantic hedge and ditch, landing without a stumble on the far side. A moment later he had turned in the deep plough beyond and was cantering back down the uncultivated track, past the steaming sieved fruit that was trickling slowly through the narrow hunting gate. No one said anything and no one followed over the boundary hedge.

No one on the other hand was riding Be Fair.

As the new year of 1970 loomed, we dared to hope that I might be able to compete in my first British Horse Society Novice One Day Event on Be Fair in the coming spring. In January, Be Fair left Tom and went to prep-school with the compliment ringing in his ears, 'the best young horse that I have ever ridden'. And that was some compliment coming from one so experienced as Tom.

The headmistress of the prep-school was still Mrs Firth but this time the aim was no longer to sort out a nappy youngster but to prepare a budding novice eventer for his first event.

By now, I attended a more lenient school and was able

to spend each week-end with the Firths, riding Be Fair and learning the first elements of event preparation.

The dressage was a joke. Be Fair was stiff and I was floppy. Very quickly he learnt that he could take advantage of my ignorance – he found that he did not have to bend his body this way and that or answer my aids if he did not feel so inclined.

At the beginning of the spring holidays in 1970, Be Fair and I were booked in for five days of lessons staying at Dick Stillwell's establishment near Wokingham in Berkshire. He had helped teach Sea Sway since I was fourteen, and I held him in great respect. I could not wait to hear what he thought of my new horse.

Mr Cook left Be Fair, me and the trailer at Dick's stables and rumbled home in the ageing Sunshine.

There were four of us in the morning's lesson and when Dick came into the covered school we were already trotting round it.

'Mawning girls,' rang out Dick's imitation-snob voice, 'and how are you awl this mawning then?' A pause and he returned to his normal voice. 'This your new young one then Lucinda is it?' He watched him for a moment. 'Um. Nice little horse, but you know something, he's not quite level behind ... in fact he's not just not level, he's downright lame.'

The horror of it – I had so looked forward to this week and relied upon it as my principal preparation before our first One Day Event. A week ago, Be Fair had given one of his hind pasterns a nasty cut on some old tin he had struck whilst riding on Salisbury Plain. We had thought he was better but obviously he was not.

Reluctantly Dick said, 'We won't win any medals working a lame horse will we? I think you'd better ring up home and get them to come and fetch you back. It'll take a day or two for him to come sound on that. No use sitting around here waiting for it.' Forlornly I led Be Fair out of the school and put him in the stable. My parents were away and I went and telephoned our wonderful German cook, Erna. I asked her to tell Mr Cook the bad news as soon as he and Sunshine returned.

The local Pony Club were trying to scratch together a team for the Pony Club interbranch showjumping competition held every spring holiday and Be Fair and I went along to join the list of possible horses and riders at the local rally. Pat Burgess, a South African, was instructing and I already knew and liked her from the days when she had helped me in the Pony Club showjumping team with Sea Sway. For lack of anyone more competent, the Pony Club had been forced to put Sea Sway and myself in the interbranch One Day Event team during our first spring together in 1968. I fell off twice across country and was eventually eliminated.

In 1969 the show-jumping team had succeeded in finding its way into the main arena at Hickstead, much to everyone's amazement and jubilation, followed swiftly by terror as we entered the great arena which was filled with over-sized obstacles. But this rally in spring 1970 was the first day Pat had met Be Fair and she was marginally horrified by the performance we put up.

She did not know what to say to me because she knew how proud I must be to be riding my own new horse. She was also under the impression that I had just spent a week with Dick Stillwell, so I must know what I was doing. However, as she watched me ask Be Fair to stand further and further back from each jump, she could not really believe that this was quite what Dick had taught me. She wondered how she could possibly make me understand that the way I was riding was heading for disaster. She did not have to explain – I asked Be Fair to take off for a jump from an impossible distance and he landed in the middle as I flew over his head.

From that day onward Pat had my implicit trust. Everything she tentatively suggested I might try, I did and as one thing after another worked for us, so the partnership between Be Fair and me began to grow.

The first time I noticed PE 123 was during the cross-country phase of our first Novice event at Rushall, that same spring. Be Fair and I were cantering steadily from fence to fence when I became aware of a whispering noise behind me. A silver-grey Rolls Royce, number plate PE 123, was undulating smoothly across the fields, watching every fence as we jumped it. Inside it the driver was Lieutenant-Colonel 'Babe' Moseley, Chairman of the Junior European Team Selection Committee. At that time he had neither run into the side of a milk float as it turned right in front of him, nor driven for six miles in the wrong direction up the M4 and therefore still had his driving licence.

Colonel Moseley's very presence sent a tremor through me. I rarely spoke to him in those days but occasionally it was unavoidable. Two weeks after Rushall he watched one of my habitually chronic dressage tests at Kilsby, the following event. I left the arena fixing my attention

Tackling our first Novice One Day Event: Rushall, 1970 (*Clive Hiles*)

Kilsby, 1970: Our second Novice event (Clive Hiles)

on nothing, in the far distance, in order to avoid his gaze. But I could not fail to hear the high-pitched voice as it made full use of an octave, 'Bi Fair ... come hiere.' In 1970 it was infrequent to find a junior under the specified age of eighteen who was riding a proper horse as opposed to an over-sized pony. For that reason, combined with Be Fair going slowly and deliberately but clear in his first three Novice events, Colonel Moseley asked us to join the fifteen other selected combinations for the trial, at Tidworth Three Day Event in May, for the Junior European Championship Team.

We had a suspicion that it might be a bit early in Be Fair's career for him to tackle a Three Day Event and we were not too sure what to do. The Firths suggested that we enter him for the Intermediate class at Sherborne in early May and use that as a barometer of his readiness to cope with Tidworth.

Nor were we entirely certain what a Three Day Event entailed. Our experience consisted of a visit to cross-country day at Tidworth the previous year. My mother had been to the Badminton Three Day Event in 1950 to watch her sister have a bit of fun with her hunter – she succeeded in negotiating the course as far as the first Luckington Lane crossing before being eliminated. I personally had only one recollection of Badminton. Some friends had taken me when I was seven and my sole memory was of standing in some ditch called a coffin, seeing horses' tummies and the soles of riders' boots as they jumped across it. I remember being infuriated because no one could explain why it was called a coffin when there was no long wooden box to be found in the ditch.

At the age of twelve, I remember, any aspirations I might have had concerning riding in a Three Day Event were blown apart by my Pony Club camp instructress.

'If you want to go Three Day Eventing,' she said, 'you have to be a very good mathematician; the timings and the distances are dreadfully complicated.' As I had failed the sixth successive maths exam at the end of that term I decided to try my hand at showjumping instead. Sunshine, driven either by my mother or Mr Cook, trailed me and my second pony Rebel, a fat dun Connemara bought from the Firths, round the local shows for a whole year. Then Sea Sway replaced Rebel and mercifully took a much greater fancy to natural timber than to coloured. So my interests were directed away from showjumping and back towards eventing. A Three Day Event however, was far more complicated than any Pony Club One Day Event experienced with Sea Sway.

We had kept last year's Tidworth programme and on studying the timetable for the speed and endurance phase, we worked out that Be Fair must be fit enough to go fifteen miles in under one and a half hours. We did know that hunting fit was not fit enough but that was the extent of our knowledge. Somehow we had to find the pieces of the jigsaw and then fit them together.

The first day of dressage and the last day of show-jumping worried us little. But somehow we had to work out how to negotiate the four consecutive phases of the second day in the allotted time, using as little of Be Fair's energy as possible. Phases A and C were roads and tracks, where careful riding and constant adherence to a watch would save much of the horse's energy. Phase B seemed to be a fast two mile gallop over about ten steeplechase fences. A ten minute halt for a vets' inspection and a refreshing wash-down for the horse formed a welcome rest before four or more miles of galloping across country, jumping over thirty fixed obstacles of all types.

We picked up all sorts of hints on how to make Be Fair fit enough. Our great friends the Borwicks, who had advised us of Tom Payne's abilities, produced some information on methods that Peter Borwick had used when he competed in the 1948 Olympic Games. My father clearly remembered how he had made his horse fit enough to win a race in Cairo in 1926. Mrs Firth was a great help too and she was more up to date with her knowledge. She had ridden round Tidworth in 1965 and that was before there was a compulsory ten minute break preceding the cross-country.

Little by little we pieced our own method together using the ingredients of several others. I returned to school and my mother was left in charge of preparing Be Fair for his debut into Three Day Events. Firstly she bought a grooming machine. Then she set out every morning for a conscientious four hour ride. Sometimes she would give him a long slow canter for ten minutes or so or a gallop if she found a big enough field.

Every week-end I returned home and practised this ridiculous dressage at which neither of us seemed to be improving very much.

During one weekend in early May we took Be Fair down to Dorset for the Sherborne Intermediate Horse Trials. He eliminated himself in the showjumping by refusing to pass the entrance until he had made his point by backing out of it during his round. He went across country with no such naughty tricks but instead with a confidence which decided us to risk his inexperience and run him at Tidworth. Another week-end the three of us, armed with pots of paint, jumped into the car and drove off to paint the countryside red. Each red cross meant a kilometre and as the car's speedometer only read miles there was little or no agreement about exactly which tree or gatepost to daub. We had been advised to practise the complicated roads and tracks timings and I went one further than the advice: on my first rehearsal I did it in full cross-country dress. In those days the villagers still looked if they saw a horse trot through their village but they positively stared when they saw a rider in a pale

Gaining confidence on the cross-country: Sherborne, 1970 (*Clive Hiles*)

'And who are you?' Be Fair meets my new puppy, Oliver Plum. Spring, 1970

yellow motor-cycle type helmet, with jersey to match, two watches on one arm and paper with timings thereon, sellotaped on the other.

Major Firth strongly advised us to practise the steeplechase phase too. He told us that few people took this phase seriously enough and if only people learnt properly how to ride a fence at speed they would take much less out of their horses.

The following two Saturdays saw Be Fair playing racehorses in the still wilderness of that part of Salisbury plain which takes its name from the only sound which fills the air, Larkhill.

I felt fear as we thundered down into our first steeplechase fence. We were going fast and the brush fence loomed up large and black and at great speed. I saw that we were on the wrong stride and I began to drop anchor and try to slow Be Fair down at the last minute to give him a chance to fiddle over it when his stride brought him too close to the fence.

'Kick girl, kick for God's sake,' reverberated Major Firth's voice across the plain, disturbing the lark's morning recreation.

It took many attempts before I could convince my arms and legs that when going at that speed it was invariably safer to accelerate into a fence and stand off it than to decelerate and try to pop over it. Be Fair's respect for Arkle must have grown by the minute; mine did certainly for that superhuman breed – the jump jockey.

Three days before Tidworth, I came out in a rash and felt awful. I thought I might have contracted German measles but I could not imagine how. I stumbled around the cross-country course on foot in the company of the other juniors, who were being aided on their walk round with advice from the Junior Team chef d'équipe, Mrs Reid.

I did not feel any better as I trotted Be Fair up at the vets' inspection the evening before the Three Day Event commenced. No one seemed to think that Be Fair was particularly sound and the vets gave a verdict of 'a bit pottery'. Colonel Babe replied in his authoritative squeak 'Let him potter on.' As far as we knew, there was nothing wrong with him, he had always trotted like that.

On the first day, Be Fair and I entered the dressage arena, described some pointless square-edged circles, cantered once on the right leg and once accidentally on the wrong leg. We stopped three yards past the appropriate point, askew across the centre line. I bowed to the judges and we left the beastly little white boards, sighing with relief. Most of the other juniors saw dressage in much the same light and no one became very steamed up about it. It was the next day, the speed and endurance day, which counted.

The German measles left me feeling wretched until I was started on phase A, then miraculously I felt better. We thoroughly enjoyed the first twenty minute period of roads and tracks, trotting and cantering along rides we had never seen before. Phase B, the steeplechase, was less amusing. I still could not feel either happy or safe at that speed. My instinctive desire to stay alive nearly let me down at the open ditch. My parents and the Firths who were watching saw only a cloud of dust as I landed and they had to wait for it to settle to see if we would emerge together or separately. Fortunately we were still as one, despite Be Fair hitting the take-off boards because I had panicked and suddenly tried to hook him back to fiddle it, instead of kicking on to stand him off.

Forty enjoyable but anxious minutes later the second Phase C – roads and tracks – was completed on time. We arrived in the 'box'. This is a roped-off area where the horses are washed down and walked around for a ten minute break. During this compulsory halt my mother and father and I washed down Be Fair ourselves and walked him around. I was thoroughly apprehensive of what seemed an enormous cross-country ahead. I wondered how Be Fair would cope and whether or not he would have enough energy to jump all thirty-two fences covering four miles.

I had avoided housework each morning at school in order to bicycle up and down a steep Cotswold hill but still I was not sure if I was fit enough either. I had vivid memories of how, during our trip last year to watch the cross-country at Tidworth, I had heard a horse coming through a wood, gasping for breath. Only when it passed me did I realise that it was not the horse but the rider who was gasping.

We went very steadily across country; Be Fair made no serious errors. My mother, my father and I were beside ourselves with delight. Be Fair really must be a

Tidworth, 1970: Our first Three Day Event and no serious errors
(*Findlay Davidson*)

Three Day Event horse. He went better across country at Tidworth than he had at any of his One Day Events during that spring. In fact we began to realise that a Three Day Event was even more fun than a One Day Event because it did not flash by so quickly and there was very much more time in which to enjoy ourselves.

The German measles, rash and all, had completely disappeared the following day. Be Fair jumped well enough in the showjumping to have only one fence down despite my habit of kicking him at the last moment to stand him back at most of the fences.

His first Three Day Event completed, he stood in eleventh position. We were delighted. Indeed we were so delighted that when Colonel Babe asked my father whether he would like Be Fair put on the end of the short-list for the 50/50 chance of going to the Junior Championships in Denmark that August, we decided to decline.

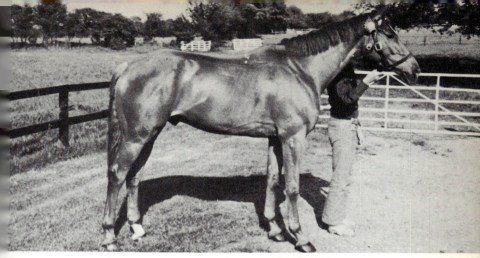

Be Fair displaying his rosette for completing Tidworth

We were beginning to realise that in Be Fair we did have a good horse. At last he seemed to be thinking less about himself and more about the job in hand. He began to enjoy everything he did more and more. We had taken a gamble competing at Tidworth so soon in his career and we did not want to risk another. We felt that he would benefit more if we spent all the following autumn event season building up our experience together in Novice One Day Events.

A week later I received a letter from the Chairman of the Selectors; I kept it by my bed at school. Few letters have given me such excitement or such incentive.

Dear Lucinda,
I fear you must have been desperately disappointed not to have been put on the short-list at Tidworth after doing so well – I am sorry about this but I believe you have a really promising horse, capable of the highest standard in the making. You rode it very well throughout but I think you agree that it is not quite ready, well though it has done. I hope that you will come forward again next year.
Yours sincerely,
R. B. Moseley.

3 Learning, Learning

It was a foregone conclusion that Be Fair and I would be in our Pony Club Interbranch One Day Event Team. We were, after all, the only members of the Royal Artillery Pony Club that had competed in a B.H.S. event, let alone reaching such heights as completing the Tidworth Three Day Event. I felt rather grand as we proceeded, with our preferred slow-beat, stately canter across country in the Area Trials, held that August at Sherborne. I thought it was all rather easy until I found it impossible to extricate my poor horse from where he lay wedged underneath a small combination fence we had tried to take in one leap across its straightforward corner. He found himself there because I was being taught the first of many lessons on attitude and technique.

'Eventing is the greatest leveller.' Never was a phrase better coined. I had my initial taste of its bitter-sweet meaning that hot summer afternoon as my team-mates and their parents abandoned their smaller and stockier beasts and came to help rescue a smart chestnut thoroughbred. They had to drag him out from under the rails by the tail, as I sat on his head to stop him struggling to rise too soon and thereby injuring himself.

A less cocky, rather apprehensive pair set off round the first Novice event of the autumn season at Eridge in mid-August. I walked the cross-country three times, so determined was I not to make another blunder like the one at Sherborne. Nonetheless, I still managed to present Be Fair at the fifth fence at the wrong angle. He hit it hard and I came off over his head. I had to give him a reminder with my whip to persuade him to jump the

'Much improved' at Kyre Novice Horse Trials, 1970 (*Clive Hiles*)

next two fences. He was beginning to lose confidence and starting to look back over his shoulder again. We were one of over 100 combinations competing and a fall was a fairly ordinary sight. No one would bother if they saw a fall, provided there was no harm done. It worried me very much though, for I felt that I had regressed to below the bottom rung. Would I pull up again? I had been worried that Tidworth was a fluke – maybe such worries were justified.

Kyre Novice Horse Trials in September raised our morale considerably. Be Fair was fifth, the best we had ever done. Mrs Reid, the Junior Team chef d'équipe, judged the dressage and wrote in the remarks column at

47

the bottom of the score sheet, 'Much improved, hope we will see you both in the Junior Team next year.' To read that unexpected comment gave me an enormous lift. Maybe big brother was not watching every move, maybe they did not know how far I had descended since Tidworth and maybe they had not lost the interest indicated in the letter of encouragement that Colonel Babe had sent me after Tidworth.

The Kyre organisers had allotted us stabling for the night with a kind person called Mrs Andrews. During the course of the evening, we discovered that her resident niece, Barby, had actually ridden her horse Sam round the Burghley Three Day Event that year and, but for a small piece of misfortune in the Bull Pens, would have been well placed. Neither my mother nor I could believe that we were staying in the same house as someone who had reached such heights. Two years later they put a plaque in their stable saying 'Be Fair slept here.'

Each event taught me a little more about riding across country and, following some improvement in the dressage with the help of the Pony Club team instructress Mrs Pinney and two lessons from Dick Stillwell, we were placed higher in each of our last two autumn Novice events.

After every cross-country round I used to feel that Be Fair had gone rather fast and wondered why we always had time faults. My mother used to wonder why we were going so slowly and was never in the least surprised that we were penalised. I suppose that I was no natural judge of pace and Be Fair was a very careful horse who liked to take his time and see what he was doing. Gradually I learnt that many of those valuable seconds were wasted as we landed over a fence, sighing with relief at what was past instead of pushing on for what was to come. With repeated reminders from Lady Hugh Russell each time we went to practise at Wylye, I began to learn the importance of a 'quick getaway' from

Cullompton Novice, 1970: Be Fair's first tentative jump into water

Tweseldown Novice, 1970: Learning to jump out (*Clive Hiles*)

Wylye Novice, 1970: Learning to jump at angles (*Clive Hiles*)

each fence. I learnt how vital it was to have an accurate line of approach on every fence that I jumped, and how time could be saved if I walked that line on foot very carefully beforehand and remembered certain trees and bundles of nettles on which to sight myself.

Aptly, Be Fair rounded off his first year of Novice eventing by coming second at Wylye Novice Horse Trials in October. He started his winter holidays as a newly upgraded Intermediate Event Horse. I had felt that he was ready to win his last Novice and had tried very hard. Since the days of my first pony, it had always been a family joke that I could never actually be first. The joke would have to continue for quite some while.

Whilst Be Fair took his winter holiday, turned out in the field each day, I was sent to France to be 'finished' and supposedly to learn French. I took with me the precious collection of photographs taken professionally at various events during the year. The arrival of any mail

THE BRITISH HORSE SOCIETY
INCORPORATING THE PONY CLUB
THE NATIONAL EQUESTRIAN CENTRE
STONELEIGH, KENILWORTH, WARWICKS.
CV8 2LR

Secretary: J. E. BLACKMORE.

Telephone: COVENTRY 27192

Date as Postmark

This is to inform you that your horse ....BE FAIR.... up-graded to Grade I/II at the ....Wylye.... Horse Trials, having won a total of £ 21 in Official B.H.S. Horse Trials.

Combined Training Secretary.

addressed to me was as exciting as it was rare but if it was a beige envelope marked 'Do not bend', then whichever one of the family saw it first, eagerly ripped it open, longing to study its contents and re-live the fun of a particular competition. Be Fair and I wrote each other letters discussing our thoughts and fancies. Be Fair's spelling of the English language was worse even than my attempts at the French one.

Darling Mum,
I am having a luverlee lazee time in the feeld riggling my bare toez in the graz. Wen r u cuming home agane coz I am longing to start awl owr fun agane.
Lots of luv
Be Fair

I returned to England just in time to fill Be Fair's stocking and creep across the frozen lawn late on Christmas Eve to leave it hanging from the bolt on his door. He had to wait until after church the next day to open it, most of which time he spent trying to nuzzle out of the way the prickly holly stuck in the top, so that he could attack the apples, carrots, polos and sugar lumps which lay wrapped in coloured tissue paper beneath.

Apart from his friend Jupiter, my aged first pony, Be Fair was alone at Appleshaw and therefore always the centre of our attention. He became an integral part of the family and we loved him as such. At times he was very spoilt but he never became vulgar or greedily expectant. He remained very choosy over whom he would talk to and even more particular as to whom he would offer his affection. Men did not appeal to him and my father was one of the few he learnt to trust over the years – Be Fair's love of Polos eventually overcame his natural reticence. Many have tried to win favour with him by feeding him titbits, but none save Daddy have succeeded. When my father came to the tackroom door to say something to me, he would feel a soft determined nudge in his back. Looking round he would see Be Fair nearly falling over his breast-bar as he stood on tip-toe in his stable, neck outstretched, big black eyes wide and innocent, head always tilted slightly to one side to gain that extra inch and look even more appealing. 'Surely you really came over to talk to *me,* didn't you?' his expression would clearly state.

After a life-time's involvement with horses, my father stood by the accepted medical fact that horses do not reason, their thought process being governed by association of ideas. Be Fair, however, flawed his belief and eventually Daddy was as convinced as the rest of the family that here was a horse who could really reason.

After Christmas I took Be Fair to Gloucestershire for a treat: a day's hunting with the Duke of Beaufort. We were following in a massive field of over 250 and, with my usual hunting fortune, no chance of a run arose to help us escape. Nonetheless we managed to distinguish ourselves: Be Fair, who hates being jostled and pushed by other horses, stopped dead in the middle of a bunch who were jumping a tiny post and rails. There was a wail of cold dissatisfaction from the lady riding side-saddle directly behind me. As I looked round to apologise I recognised under the customary black veil of a side-saddle habit the face of the Duchess of Beaufort. I wondered if we would ever be allowed back to 'Beaufortshire'.

The following week I took him for one more treat, this time to the V.W.H. Hunt. He was surprisingly placid and seemed to be feeling the cold, for he stood trembling a little by the covert-side. Slightly suspicious of his well-being, I brought him home early. The next day he stood miserably in the back of his stable, head low and shivering, despite all the blankets I had wrapped him up in. The vet came and diagnosed the flu – a virus. He also discovered that Be Fair was anaemic. Apparently chestnuts are prone to anaemia and we found that it was a condition which recurred throughout his life. However, apart from a persistent cough, within three weeks all signs of illness had disappeared.

Since the autumn we had been worrying about Be Fair's unlevelness. His dressage test sheets frequently stated that he was not level behind. Two vets who examined him thought that he might have fallen over backwards, rearing as a youngster. This could have caused some slight damage to his pelvis which had prevented adequate muscle development on the off-side, thus preventing completely level movement. Others had advised us to have his back looked at in case a misplaced vertebra might be causing the trouble.

During late January 1971, whilst Be Fair was limited to slow work as a result of his cough, we thought it a good opportunity to take him to Mr Mactimmony. He was recommended to us as 'the one man in England who really understands about backs'. He had trained several others to take on his work and rarely saw patients himself any more. However, my father persuaded him to stop at the Weston Manor Hotel near Bicester, on his way to the races. There, it was arranged, he should meet Be Fair whom we would unload in the coach yard at the back of the hotel.

Shortly after Sunshine's arrival, a very long, white car pulled into the coach yard. The door opened and a diminutive man climbed out, sporting a black French artist's beret on his balding head. My mother and I were surprised by his stature and his gentleness. We had expected a tall man, bulging with muscles and blinding us with osteopathic science. He introduced himself to us and then to Be Fair, with whom he purposefully spent a few minutes, gaining his trust. He then stepped onto a straw bale that he had asked us to bring and began his examination and a manipulation of Be Fair's back. He found three misplaced vertebrae, which he quietly but firmly knocked back into position. He did not manipulate through strength. No human being is strong enough to move the spine of a mature horse by force. He explained that he worked on the same principle as knocking a jam-jar lid that had stuck, or a drawer that was wedged, neither of which could be moved by the direct application of strength.

By chance we mentioned that Be Fair had a cough which seemed unending. Mr Mactimmoney began to feel his axis – the point where the head joins the neck. With a quick jerk and another check-up, he told us that Be Fair would no longer cough. Apparently a small displacement of the axis was causing it to press on a nerve, which caused irritation of the sinus. Before he had even finished his explanation, both Be Fair's nostrils started to stream with thick white phlegm. The stream continued for half an hour. Although for the rest of his life he had a suspicion of a dry cough, to all intents and purposes the cough which the virus had left him with, was cured.

One of the first of many wise pieces of advice that Dick Stillwell imparted was while he was teaching me on Sea Sway in the early days:
'Never stay in one place, Lucinda. Go and learn as much as you can from as many different people as'll teach you.' Frequently to this day I find that someone might have been telling me something for literally years but it will only sink in when another says exactly the same thing in a different way, maybe merely by using a fresh simile.

Princess Anne was beginning to emerge into the world of eventing and my mother and I had both noticed how well schooled her horses were. Early in the New Year my mother asked Princess Anne's trainer, Alison Oliver, if she would help Be Fair and I to learn some dressage. She agreed and Be Fair was sent a week in advance to learn some lessons, so that it would not be an outright case of the blind leading the blind. When I joined him I was secretly rather annoyed to discover that Alison had only ridden him once during that week and that the young man who was working for her had ridden him for the rest of the time. The young man's name was David Hunt.

We stayed there for the last two weeks of February 1971, during which time my inadequacies in this sphere produced frustration and despondency. I had never thought myself a particularly able exponent of dressage but I did not think that I compared too unfavourably with those event competitors about me. At Alison's I suffered for the first time the humiliation of watching Be Fair going well for her and David but not for me. Whenever I tried his back hollowed, his head went up and he started accidently to misunderstand all I asked. I was indeed blind to the art of dressage and so presumably was Be Fair. Nonetheless he had a clear view of which garden path he should lead me up.

My respect for David inevitably grew and as he was nearer my age I did not feel such a fool when I tried to ride in front of him. Alison was extremely busy with many other clients, particularly with her royal protégé, and so a mutual decision was made and Alison, no doubt thankfully, handed me over to David.

With three more days of my fortnight left, Be Fair still went along with his nose stuck out, most of the time bending his neck towards the walls of the covered school instead of towards the inside. I felt that I had neither achieved anything nor even made any intelligent progress, especially now I knew that Be Fair was not physically incapable of lowering his naturally high head carriage and doing what he was asked to do. That third to last morning I had a lesson at 10.30 am. By 1.00 pm I had still made no impression on Be Fair. David, seeing my look of despair, encouraged me to carry on trying, saying he would come back after lunch. Soon we were alone in the school, with no one watching to give me a complex as I struggled vainly to find the key. Some time after lunch, David returned to find that for the first time Be Fair had lowered his head for me and begun to stretch out his neck, more through exhaustion than any skill of mine. This breakthrough was certainly not the end of all our troubles, for I understood much too little to take full advantage of it. It was, however, a beginning and after that, when I was trying to school him, Be Fair seemed to notice that there was in fact someone on his back.

Fortunately we did not have to plunge straight into an Intermediate class at the beginning of the 1971 spring season. Firstly we completed the Novice course at Crookham, the preliminary Trial for the Junior European Team Championships.

While I was trotting rather fast in jagged circles, in other words warming up for the dressage, Richard Meade, Mexico Team gold medallist, rode past and said 'Good morning.' I was sure that he could not be addressing me and looked over my shoulder to see who was behind me. A few minutes later he rode up beside me as Be Fair walked on a loose rein in a bigger circle. He asked about Be Fair and chatted about his progress. I could not think what to say to him, so I asked, 'What's that you're riding?' I was not quite sure whether to add Mr Meade or Richard, so I added nothing.

'It's The Poacher,' he answered; together they had won Badminton the year before.

I told my mother of the flattery of having the great Golden Boy himself speak to me. I also told her that I feared his interest in Be Fair might only be because he had his eye on him to ride himself. We began to entertain horrible thoughts of being offered so much for him that we would be unable to refuse. For the remainder of that year I regarded with the utmost suspicion any encouragement or help that poor Richard was, in fact, simply offering to us as one of many promising young English combinations.

Although unplaced at Crookham, Be Fair made the Novice cross-country feel easy. It was time to graduate to the next stage. In early April Rushall was once again our launching pad, this time into Intermediate classes. The dressage was fair and the showjumping and cross-country very satisfactory. He gained seventh place, as he had done there the previous year in his first Novice class.

The next day I found a soft lump three inches below the point of his near-hock. It looked suspiciously as if a curb was trying to form. Hot kaolin and cold hosing was repeated for a few days and, instead of turning into the hard, bony enlargement of a curb, it disappeared completely, never to reappear. It was a happy reminder of the old adage: a stitch in time saves nine.

We fitted in three more events of Intermediate standard before Tidworth in May. One of them was Sherborne. There, at a fence about ten yards from the corner of last year's incident during the Pony Club trials, another lesson was learned. It was a stark 'island fence', of post and rails, at the bottom of a steep bracken-covered hill. Behind the fence the ground dropped sharply away for three to four feet before flattening out. We were moderately collected, having made a steady descent of the steep hill, and I could see that we were on the wrong stride for the fence. Instead of sitting still and holding and balancing him, I committed a crime which is perhaps the commonest fault among all jump riders: I panicked, lessened the contact from the reins and kicked him to stand back, throwing my body forward to encourage him to take off. I might have escaped trouble if it had not been for the drop. I learnt that horses will rarely stand off a fence when the landing is unsighted. Accordingly it is best not to ask them to. Unbalanced by my shifting weight and slackened rein, Be Fair put in another stride, hit the fence half way up his front legs and catapulted me to the bottom of the bank. He never fell himself.

The ice-cream van, complete with navigator – Oliver Plum

Shortly after I had passed my driving test, Sunshine and the trailer were swopped for a cream-coloured Lambourn Caravella, a two-horsebox we called the 'ice-cream van'. It was under three tons which meant that I could drive it.

Be Fair, Oliver Plum, my impossibly disobedient Cavalier Spaniel, and myself set out for our next event, the Windsor Horse Trials in early May, all on our own for the first time, in the ice-cream van. At last I was independent. I was so proud to be alone with Be Fair and entirely responsible for him. When I was walking the course, I met Derek Allhusen, an old 9th Lancer friend of my father's, who had won an Individual silver medal in Mexico. He kindly offered to walk the whole course again with me. This was one of many times he took specific trouble to advise me in some way or another.

A beastly jump into the edge of a lake proved to be most people's Waterloo. The lake became shoulder deep three strides after landing and only a few people managed to turn and wade out before they went out of their depth and found themselves swimming. Be Fair was one of many who received a ducking as a reward for a big, bold entry jump. Somehow we emerged, soaking wet but still together, from our unscheduled aquatic venture. Be Fair continued around the course with his left ear stuck out horizontally from his head. He was trying to drain it of water. It was my first experience of jumping with reins, saddle, breeches and boots wet and slippery. I almost fell off with the slight jar on the landing side of the next drop fence. Four fences later I did fall off. My inaccurate line into a corner fence made Be Fair refuse. I flew over his head and over the corner as well; another lesson learnt but a definite increase in my animosity for corners.

Colonel Babe happened to patter past me at the end of the day. He did not say much but his meaning was clear.

'Hum. Be Fair and you have not had a very impressive record lately, have you?' He spoke slowly in his high-pitched crisp voice. 'You will have to pull your socks up at Tidworth, young girl, if you are to convince me that you are worthy of being in my team.'

The clear progress which I had thought I could foresee, culminating in being a member of the Junior Team to go to Germany in July, looked distinctly blurred. In his unique way, Colonel Babe sensed that I was complacently allowing myself to run downhill. Such was my respect for that great man that a sentence from him, tinged with displeasure, was enough to sharpen my attitude.

Tidworth drew closer and my apprehension grew stronger. I studied even more closely the article on horse fitness that I had cut out earlier in the spring. Sheila Willcox's methods seemed to suit Be Fair better than the one we ourselves had evolved for him the previous year, when he had become dull and lethargic in the latter stages of the season. I halved the four hours exercise a day and increased the fast work each week until the programme concluded with a one and a half mile gallop at three-quarter speed. I presumed that this meant not flat out but nearly.

We had heard that there was an awesome Trakhener fence on the cross-country course at Tidworth: a lone telegraph pole slung above a wide, deep ditch at the base of a hill. The thought of Be Fair having to jump this filled me with increasing horror until eventually, two days before the Three Day Event was due to commence, I could bear it no longer and took Be Fair down to Lady Hugh Russell at Wylye in order to practise jumping some similar fences.

The idea of practising most probably was right. The timing of it was definitely wrong. Trepidation prevented me from kicking as hard as was necessary to counteract the decelerating effect that the sight of a ditch had on Be Fair. He stopped in front of the first one and then took off with his front legs. His back legs found it impossible to follow and the fronts of his stifles crashed against the unbending telegraph pole. No immediate ill effect was apparent and we were able to continue the practice, until my heels had learnt their job, and Be Fair kept up the momentum as he jumped.

The next day was Wednesday. Thursday evening was the preliminary vets' inspection at Tidworth. I decided to take Be Fair for a ride before I tried some dressage. He felt a little strange as he walked down the drive. Once on the road I trotted him to see if all was well. He proved to be so lame at trot that I was sure he had injured his back very badly indeed. He appeared locked on one side of his body. In answer to our emergency call, Mr Mahon the vet arrived within an hour. I waited to hear the worst. Already visions were running through my mind of Be Fair having to be put down.

It transpired that the damage was no more than severe bruising of his stifle joint. With half-hourly hot and cold blanket-poulticing during the next thirty-six hours we had a 50/50 chance of producing him sound for the vet's inspection. My mother and I took it in turn to perform these ablutions and by 4.30 on Thursday afternoon, much to our surprise and intense relief, Be Fair was sound and passed the vets' inspection.

Paralysed from a fall out hunting some years ago, Lady Hugh Russell 'walks' the course in a mini-moke. More often than not the moke is littered with competitors, all wanting to listen in to the advice she has to offer on lines and approaches to fences. Bumping and jostling, the moke brought us to the lip of the hill which led down to the mammoth Trakhener. Lady Hugh knew what I would be feeling about this fence after the traumas of the last few days. As she neared the dreaded fence she said, 'Lucinda, you see that chestnut tree over in the fence-line of the field, the other side of the Trakhener? Well, you keep your eyes fixed on its highest branches from the moment you come over the brow of the hill. Don't, whatever you do, look down at the ditch – just stare at those branches and keep kicking.'

A picture of that chestnut tree is still clearly imprinted on my mind; by the time we were soaring across the Trakhener I felt I knew the shape of every branch on its trunk. It was wise advice from Lady Hugh and it led to the formation of an important brick in the wall of confidence that Be Fair and I were building around us.

Lord and Lady Hugh Russell with their 'moke'

In the showjumping phase on the third day of Tidworth, we threw away a chance of winning by knocking down one showjump. Instead, Tony Hill on Chicago picked up the honours, but we were nonetheless thoroughly content with third place and our joke about never managing to actually win continued.

Fearful that the ducking Be Fair had received at Windsor might have made him lose confidence about jumping into water, we decided that we must find a similar situation in which to practise. There was nowhere locally and we could think of only one solution.

One morning in early July Be Fair and I were much surprised to find ourselves jumping into the lake at Badminton. We had been given permission to practise over the old log at the water's edge, which was no longer used in competition. After several unhesitating splash downs, Be Fair's confidence with water jumps was confirmed and I took him for a walk to dry him off.

I remember the thrill I felt as I rode around that beautiful park in the height of summer – the quietness, the blending colours of the trees, beneath whose leaf-crowded arms the deer took refuge from the sun. I pretended for a moment that I was actually a competitor at the Badminton Horse Trials. I felt that I must savour every minute because although I longed to compete there, I deemed it most unlikely.

Although very enthusiastic, I was reluctant to be ambitious. I could imagine ourselves in the Junior Team but I could not see us advancing beyond that stage. Riding out with a fellow competitor at Alison Oliver's one day, I remember being told that the top was a closed shop.

'They aren't a very friendly lot. I gather that they are cold and jealous and don't encourage anyone to join them. It's impenetrable territory up there you know.'

The final team trial for the 1971 Junior European Championships took place at Wing in Buckinghamshire that July. It was won by Olive Oyl, the little dun who was no more than a pony from Northern Ireland, who had won the Junior Trial at Tidworth the previous year. Be Fair was second. These two and four others made up the Junior European Championship Team. In late July they set sail for Germany in a smart white horsebox with a horizontal red stripe; the riders were transported in a matching mini-bus. It was my first taste of the special intimacy and excitement associated with travelling overseas with one's much-loved horse.

The day after we and the horses had arrived at Wesel, near Munster, PE 123 whispered its way through the town and found the big Dutch barn in which horses from all the visiting teams were installed. Much to our horror, they were not in stables but in narrow stalls, where they did not have enough room to lie down.

Colonel Babe and his selectors had decided on the team's order of running. First Andy Brake and Say When, then Be Fair, Mandy Sivewright and Gameel, and last to go would be Olive Oyl and Chris Brooke. The evening prior to the competition we were each given a white saddle-cloth with a Union Jack on either side. I showed it to Be Fair, in the hope that it would induce a patriotic instinct which might help him behave in the dressage. He obviously did not recognise a Union Jack when he saw one for he paid not the slightest attention to me during the entire dressage test. Instead, he stared about him, spooking at the judges' boxes at one end and becoming unexpectedly fascinated in horticulture as he studied intently the geraniums which bordered the rest of the arena. The best three scores in each team count and Britain lay third behind West Germany and France after the dressage. Be Fair's dressage score was the discard of the British Team.

The cross-country was well built and not very difficult except for fence three, the Bootsweg. A steep downhill

Dreadful dressage in the Junior European Championships, Wesel, 1971; Be Fair ignoring all my directions (*Mitschke*)

approach preceded a steeper table at the edge of a small lake. I was glad to have the practice at Badminton under our belt, though I did not dare tell anyone that I had been there. An enthusiastic member of the British contingent decided to wade through this innocuous-looking pond before the competition began. He returned a little later rather damp. It transpired that there was a line of old shell holes running across the water's bed on the left and very deep mud lay on the right. There was only one safe place to jump in order to avoid both these traps. The Germans and the French knew it and so did we. A large number of competitors from other nations did not and were duly submerged or bogged down. Mandy's glue was thoroughly tested as Gameel veered right and struggled to regain his sinking feet. Olive Oyl enjoyed traditional Irish luck as he jumped left and missed all the

Fence three, the Bootsweg: Wesel

holes. Be Fair on the other hand, showed his team-mates how to do it as he jumped without any hesitation, keeping to exactly the right line and continued clear round the course. A glass of champagne stood waiting for anyone who came through the finish of the cross-country, whether they were wet, muddy or otherwise.

Cross-country day ended leaving the competition on a knife edge for Sunday's showjumping. The French team led the English by six points at the start of the final phase. Our first team member to jump that afternoon was Andy. He had a bad ride on a rather sore Say When and knocked two down. The first Frenchman on the other hand, went clear. Say When's score would have to be the discard if the team was to have a chance. It was vital that Be Fair should do a clear round to keep the pressure

Wonderful cross-country: Wesel (*Findlay Davidson*)

on France. Having walked the course five times that morning, I could easily have ridden round it blindfold. Unfortunately I was not allowed such comfort and had to see every fence as it loomed up, wondering if we would clear it or not. Be Fair tried his hardest; he jumped clear and the excitement rose. The next Frenchman had a fence down and Britain was on top. Then Mandy and Gameel tipped one and the French Number 3 went clear. The French were back on top. Oh the agony of watching and waiting! It took over one and a half hours for the competition to end. Eventually it was Olive Oyl's turn. We held our breaths, he had to go clear. Olive flew round without a worrying moment and left a narrow-shouldered sixteen-year-old French boy to bear the heavy responsibility of having to produce a clear round if

France was to win the individual and clinch the team titles.

Be Fair and I had returned to the horsebox after watching Olive and were unable to see the arena. I heard clapping and presumed the French boy had finished his round. Had he or had he not gone clear? A crackle from the loudspeaker and a stutter of German did not help to answer my question – the torture of not being able to understand. As the commentary stopped I grasped the last word: 'punkte' meaning 'faults'. He must have had one or more down. I threw my arms round Be Fair and hugged and hugged him. I could not believe that we were in the winning Junior European Team. Britain had never before won the Junior Three Day Event Championships. None of the pundits in England had thought the team could possibly win as they were not considered to be up to the Continental standard.

Olive Oyl, who had won the individual, led the team in for the prize-giving. The loudspeaker boomed something incomprehensible across the ring ending with, '... Gross Britanien' and the band struck up with the National Anthem. Watching the Union Jack as it crept slowly up the flag pole, well ahead of the German and French flags, made me acutely proud to be British. I had never before felt even a little patriotic. Be Fair and I, although only eleventh individually, had played a small part in producing a result of which the country, not just my relations, could be proud.

Be Fair relished this, his first opportunity to show Europeans just how badly-behaved a highly-strung English thoroughbred can be. He would not stand still to have his rosette pinned on. The Mayor of Wesel spoke to him as he presented the prizes.

'Aah. I can zee zat you are not accustomed to vinning – you vill have to learn it.'

As our team began the lap of honour I caught sight of Colonel Babe. A rare but radiant smile stretched across

Colonel 'Babe' Moseley, radiant, as he holds the prize for his Junior European Champions (*Findlay Davidson*)

his round face as he stood in the arena, balancing on his tummy the prize for his Junior European Champions. The trophy symbolised the fruits of his four years of labour.

4 Out of the Nursery

WELCOME CONQUERING HEROES WELL DONE
CONGRATULATIONS

This telegram, sent by the B.H.S., awaited the victorious team at Harwich docks.

Seven telegrams and several letters awaited Be Fair and me at home. *The Horse and Hound* carried a picture of the team and a glowing report. Be Fair had never had his picture in print before let alone in the *Horse and Hound*. Previously our names had only been mentioned once or twice in connection with Junior Team Trials. I received a letter from Pat Burgess, saying that she knew she must lose me now to those more competent to teach, but should I ever need a bit of local help with some small problem I was to give her a ring. Little did she know how many hours would be spent on the telephone in the coming years, either planning future training or dissecting past performances.

The excitement of having broken through the barrier of mediocrity to face actual victory! I remember having an aching jaw by the end of that showjumping day in Wesel, merely from smiling too broadly for too long. It was unbelievable that what I had never dared to dream of had actually taken place.

Be Fair felt like a chestnut tree whose candles had sprung abruptly into bloom. He knew what he had done. I do not think it is the rosette that indicates to a horse when he has done well, but the jubilation which surrounds him. Intelligent horses seem to have a well developed extra sense which is strongly affected by the atmosphere in which they live.

'It's only early August, we can't just leave Be Fair in the field until Christmas can we? He's really fit, sound as a bell, and his legs are super. Why don't we give him a short break now and then see if we can go over to Ireland for the Punchestown Three Day Event at the end of September?'

The family discussed this possibility late on the evening of our return as we sat in the dining room over an empty champagne bottle.

Be Fair was given two weeks holiday in the field. A friend and I climbed into an Aeroflot Illushyn jet and joined a party of forty Cosmos package tourists on a fourteen day sightseeing trip to Moscow, Leningrad and Kiev. Marita and I had hatched this idea months before as we both felt an urge to see what life was like behind the Iron Curtain. In Kiev we walked across the sunburnt grass of an attractive park, whose pavilions and grounds housed examples of the advanced economic achievements of the Ukraine. I could not have foreseen that I was to return to that same park two years hence. This time not with the Cosmos party for company, but with Be Fair.

A week after returning from Russia, I drove up to Burghley to watch the cross-country phase of the European Championships. In the morning, I walked the course and was struck by the enormity of the obstacles as compared with those that I was accustomed to studying. As I measured myself against the alternative quick route through the Bull Pens, a massive parallel constructed of six telegraph poles, I sincerely wondered why I was becoming so enthusiastic about eventing. Should I ever succeed, it was plain that my reward would be to face obstacles of these horrific dimensions. The thought made my knees knock together but I felt better when I realised thankfully that the likelihood of succeeding to that degree was very slim.

For the first half of the competition, I was allotted a job as messenger by Colonel Babe. I stood with him by one of the more difficult fences and after he had studied every sixth competitor jump, I ran with his information the half mile back to the box – the fenced-in enclosure where the horses are washed down before they start on Phase D: the cross-country. Here the riders also rest for ten minutes as they are briefed on how the course is riding. I handed the notes to the British chef d'équipe, a white moustached Colonel whose benign smile, I was to learn, clothed a quick and determined brain. During the time that I was messenger, I heard that Mike Tucker's horse, Farmer Giles, had dropped dead after the steeplechase phase. I only had to put myself in Mike's place and imagine it was Be Fair who had died, and I left Burghley far from certain where my ambitions lay, or indeed if I had any at all.

The following week-end in mid-September my mother, father, Be Fair, Oliver Plum and myself set off for Devon to stay with my uncle for the Cullompton One Day Event. We felt we ought to complete an Open Intermediate course before going to Ireland because Punchestown's cross-country was bound to be more severe than Wesel's had been.

Although the alarm clock woke me early on the morning of the event the sun was already peeping through the curtains. I had been only half asleep for the past hour, and I felt more excited than usual though I was not quite sure why. As I tip-toed down a creaking oak staircase, I heard a voice in my head say something I had not heard it say before:

'I think that you might win today. I think that if you keep your head things will go right and you could win.'

I ran across the yard to tell Be Fair of this foreign notion that had crossed my mind without warning. He would not eat his breakfast – he knew something too. As I began to plait him, I told him in detail about the cross-country course. I explained everything to him, starting from where he should take off over the first fence and finishing with where he should land over the last. Since our first event together, I had explained the course to him each time. I had always told Sea Sway what to expect too. A wonderful way of crystallising plans in your own mind is to memorise them out loud to someone whom they affect as much as yourself. Be Fair loved to listen just as he loved to be 'tarted-up' before a competition. He would lower his head and half close his eyes. If I tensed my voice in describing a fence that I was either afraid of or wanted him to pay particular attention to then his eyes would open wider and he would raise his head a few inches. That morning I told him my plans twice over. Finally I stood on a bucket in front of his head stretching up to plait his forelock. He always found it amusing to make it difficult for me to reach this. If I became angry and told him crossly to lower his head then he had won. If I remained for long enough balancing on tip-toe, the blood draining out of my upstretched arms, I had won and my prize would be a condescending lowering of the head. I had learnt not to say 'Tee hee, I won that one,' because he would promptly throw his head back up, knocking me off the bucket and, more often than not, the needle out of my hand.

That morning we were on a thoroughly good wavelength and I risked being knocked off my bucket by threatening him with being forbidden to even start the cross-country if he did not behave in the dressage and make up for Wesel's embarrassing display.

In those days he must still have believed this threat and with a lesson from David only a few days behind us, he performed a very creditable test at Cullompton. I made the mistake of riding too carefully in the show-jumping phase. Be Fair was not quite sure why he was being slowed up so much in front of each fence and hit one as he found he had inadequate impulsion to jump clearly out of the double.

> **THE BRITISH HORSE SOCIETY**
> INCORPORATING THE PONY CLUB
> THE NATIONAL EQUESTRIAN CENTRE
> STONELEIGH, KENILWORTH, WARWICKS.
> CV8 2LR
>
> Secretary: J. R. BLACKMORE.
> Telephone: COVENTRY 27192
>
> Date as Postmark
>
> This is to inform you that your horse ......BE FAIR...... up-graded to Grade I/♣ at the ...Cullompton... Horse Trials, having won a total of £..71.... in Official B.H.S. Horse Trials. (Out of Intermediate classes from Everingham/Tweseldown onwards)
>
> Combined Training Secretary.

Be Fair becomes an Advanced event horse

A little flame of battle lit within me. The few marks advantage we had gained in the dressage had been thrown away by riding the showjumping over-cautiously and therefore badly. There was only one alternative left: to put my foot down across country.

Be Fair received the message loud and clear and completed a faultless round in the style which would become familiar to those who watched him in his later and greater days. It was, however, the first time we had really moved from the nursery into the drawing room. It was the first time we had gone across country without that extra caution and yet without being ensnared by a heedless disregard for the fences. It is surely this mixture that produces the best cross-country performance and it is a fine line to trace. Many times since then we have wavered either to one side or the other.

The jinx was broken; Be Fair and I had actually won our very first event by a margin of four points. Mike Bullen should have been second but he forgot to weigh in at the end of the cross-country and was eliminated. It seemed ridiculous that a man as tall as Mike, who must have weighed fourteen stone stripped, should be robbed of second place for not proving at the moment he finished that his weight was in excess of the required eleven stone eleven pounds. Rules do not flex.

The next morning we spent relaxing in my uncle's field. The hot September sun beat down on us, as we lay stretched out under the ha-ha in front of the oak-beamed Elizabethan house. Be Fair was loose in the same field, wandering nonchalantly through patches of tall grass, picking at a thistle head or a dandelion leaf, as he roamed. He must have sensed the mood for he came within ten yards of where we were sunbathing, and stood swishing his tail at the flies, musing over us for a while before lying down himself and nibbling at the daisies around his folded knees. His thoroughbred instincts do not allow him to be tamed like a dog and he will always be wary of human beings, never liking to be caught off his guard in a compromising position. That morning, however, he relaxed his defenses for ten minutes to join in the family contentment over his first individual achievement.

Four days later at the end of September and only five weeks after his last nautical trip, Be Fair was on the boat bound for Dublin. Punchestown proved to be full of as much Irish fun and laughter as was to be expected.

Punchestown Three Day Event, 1971. We sped round the steeplechase, 45 seconds inside the time limit

Extravagant jumping at Punchestown. Be Fair did not take a stride between the first set of rails and the ditch. We were becoming very confident...

Be Fair's confidence in himself was swelling rapidly and I shared it with him although the vet at the vets' inspection did not. He looked at Be Fair's long, spindly fore-legs and did not expect to see him lined up for the final inspection before the showjumping on the Sunday. He felt that such legs would not prove strong enough to withstand the strain of a Three Day Event.

With our newly acquired accelerator foot we sped around the steeplechase forty-five seconds inside the time. Later on in the day, after a lovely cross-country round filled with extravagant jumping, I was given a rocket by Colonel Babe for going at such an unnecessary speed on Phase B, the steeplechase.

'If you are three-quarters of a minute inside the time limit, it is too much. When Be Fair has a testing cross-country course ahead instead of a flat Irish bog with

Intermediate size fences across it, he will need that extra energy which you have expended on the steeplechase.'

I felt suitably squashed, but I understood the meaning of what he was saying. It made sense. No one had told me not to go too fast because never before had I gone fast enough. I filed the information away under 'S' for steeplechase.

By Sunday morning's vets' inspection Be Fair was holding third position. The vet had raised an eyebrow and said nothing as he felt Be Fair's ice-cold legs with their hard and clean tendons.

There was a parallel off a tight turn in the show-jumping, whose line of approach I walked nine times. If I could go clear there was a good chance that I would pull up to second place. It was the only fence on the course that we knocked down and with it went relegation to fourth place. Nonetheless a happy party squeezed itself into the ice-cream van and sailed for home across the Irish sea. We had given a lift to Gameel and Pammy Sivewright in order to halve the costs, and they had done very well to be second. We dropped them off at their home in Cirencester and Oliver Plum managed to be dropped off too. When I arrived home and realised one of the party was missing, for one awful moment I thought he might still be in Ireland.

After a One Day Event, a Two Day Event and two Three Day Events all within eight weeks of each other, most experienced people would think it prudent to finish eventing their horse for that season. We were not experienced enough to do so and after giving him a ten day break we decided to take a brave step and declare Be Fair to compete in the Midland Bank Open Championships of Great Britain at Wylye in mid-October. Considering the confident manner in which Be Fair had coped with his last three events, we felt that he might be ready to tackle Badminton the following year. First, however, we thought he must be introduced to an Advanced course –

how he coped with this would show us whether to plan the 1972 spring season with Badminton in view or not, so we entered him for the Championships at Wylye.

At the end of September, I was sent to cooking school in London for three months and a great friend, Wanna Pertwee, brought her own horse Bo'sun to Appleshaw. She rode and looked after Be Fair for me, to keep him in tune for the forthcoming Championships.

My cookery teacher gave me permission to omit learning how to make Cocquilles St Jacques and Rhum Baba and I took the Friday prior to the Championships off to go home and prepare Be Fair and myself for the competition. I found him in great spirits but I noticed how he had lost much of the condition that he had had before Punchestown. He definitely looked 'well hunted' and not altogether surprisingly after his busy season. He was growing his winter coat and I had to blanket-clip him which did not enhance his appearance. I would have preferred to clip all of his coat but he had a cold winter holiday ahead and he would be needing at least some of his winter woollies then.

Wylye is the one place in England to be avoided if it is stormy. The event's nucleus is situated on the top of the bleakest of downs, around which the cross-country course is built in a series of rises and descents as it sweeps the encircling steep sides of the valley.

There was not a storm on 16 October, but a monsoon. The water poured from the skies all day. Wind drove the rain into every dry niche. Horse-boxes, stuck securely in the mud, were dotted across the side of the downs. Miserable-looking horses moved sideways against sudden squalls that sent litter bins bobbing from tent to tent. For once the dressage judges were envied. They kept dry in their cars as they peered between windscreen wipers at competitors who sloshed and skidded around the arena. Be Fair and I scored nearly double the penalties of the eventual winner that day.

I was wet and cold and had evidently switched off because I let Be Fair slide to a halt in the showjumping in front of the smallest fence which was near the entrance to the arena. Be Fair made it clear that he would prefer to go home but at least he did not embarrass me by starting to nap and continued his round without further incident. Nonetheless I was worried.

'He does not stop nowadays,' I thought. 'What's up?'

That refusal was probably the best thing that could have happened. It snapped me out of my sodden lethargy. I discussed with myself the possibilities of withdrawing before the cross-country and wondered what lay at stake if I did. Badminton or no Badminton. All right, I would go across country and I would ride. If I felt he was not right in himself, then I would pull him up after the first few fences and retire.

The whole calibre and structure of an Advanced course, particularly a Championship one, bore no resemblance to anything we had met so far. It was not simply an enlarged version of an Open Intermediate, as I had always imagined. It had been built with the intention of revealing the best One Day Event horse in Great Britain. It did not remind me of any course I had jumped, only of one I had seen jumped – Badminton.

The second fence was a straightforward but vast hayrack. The leap Be Fair gave sent the same sensation through me that I had felt the first time I had jumped him at Hagley Hall. Galloping up and down the valley he devoured each fence as he met it. I was not certain of the qualities and capabilities essential to a Badminton horse, but half way round I decided that the horse I was riding must be quite close to one. I began to wonder why I had been so anxious and pent up before I had started. I began to think that this big advanced stuff was surprisingly uncomplicated. That thought, no doubt, signalled complacency and relaxation to Be Fair and caused us to have our first proper fall. A solid sleeper spread fence

... too confident. Complacency caused our first proper fall: Wylye, 1971
(*Clive Hiles*)

with a false ground-line, named the Griffin's Grotto, lay in wait for us at the top of a steep hill. We ambled uphill to the fence in fourth gear; sensing that Be Fair was a bit tired I felt sorry for him and never bothered to change into third and give him the help he needed by pulling him up together and riding into the fence. Another lesson was delivered; this time we were both quite lucky to be unharmed and still able to digest it.

We finished the course with wide smiles and big pats. My fellow competitors could not understand why I was so exhilarated when they saw that both of us were plastered in Wylye mud. I recalled Colonel Babe's letter of encouragement that he had written to me after my first Tidworth Three Day Event. 'A really promising horse capable of the highest standard in the making.' I began to think that maybe there was more than just a grain of truth in what he had written.

Unwillingly I returned to the kitchen classroom and promptly started to concoct Be Fair's plan of attack on Badminton, instead of some wretched soufflé which always collapsed before the teacher arrived to accord it a mark. At Christmas time I advertised my newly acquired cooking expertise in *Horse and Hound*. My parents had sent me on this expensive course because they felt it was the only job I could combine with eventing Be Fair. I thought I had better make an effort to justify the expense.

One unsuspecting family did risk me for a week-end party for Newbury Races. It was in the winter of the miners' strike and the ensuing powercuts – my Cordon Bleu course had not taught me how to feed a joint uncooked. It was an agonising week-end. The family were very kind and understanding and referred to me as the galloping cook. I felt however that I would prefer the anxiety and apprehension of any cross-country course in the world rather than that of cooking for another party of hungry strangers.

5 Kick on

The spring of 1972 heralded the start of the eventing season as the air began to tense with the first flushes of Olympic fever.

Crookham and the following three Advanced One Day Events were all important because we would see in action the potential Olympic combinations. But Badminton, of course, was of ultimate significance. There, according to the *Horse and Hound* (April), Lieutenant-Colonel Frank Weldon, twice winner of this, the greatest of all Three Day Events, would build a suitably awesome course to 'sort out the sheep from the goats for Britain's Olympic team'.

Every horsy magazine I opened did its best to stir up excitement and expectancy. It may not have worried the old campaigners but it certainly had the desired effect on me. Be Fair must also have sneaked a look and become nervous. He began to be very difficult to feed, constantly changed his mind about what he liked and behaved altogether as fussily as an aged aunt. Badminton suddenly seemed very close and yet, as these articles and reports filtered through my mind, the possibility of negotiating it lessened by the minute.

None of us had appreciated that 1972 would be Olympic year when we first considered competing at Badminton. We now realised that it was obviously Badminton's responsibility to sort out a team that could bring home the Gold Medal. Dear God, had I bitten off more than I could chew? Be Fair's progress had been copybook for the last two years. We had given each other a long time in which to learn. Were we going to ruin all the months of groundwork by attempting Badminton before we were ready?

No one could promise that we would not ruin him, but everyone we asked felt it was a legitimate step to take.

'If you don't do Badminton this year, what else will you do with him? You must continue to advance; you can't just do Tidworth for the third time, it won't teach either of you anything,' they all said. Their confidence helped, but I felt they were forgetting that the jockey wore an L-plate as well as the horse. It was this combination of ignorance that I feared would lead to our undoing. Secretly, I entered for Tidworth in case everything should go wrong at Badminton.

Be Fair had taken a long time to recover the condition he lost through his long autumn season, so long in fact that in January we had him tested for lung-worm. It proved negative. After three months of rest and good food, we had imagined that he would be blooming. It took another whole month before I was no longer ashamed of him and could begin his canter-work in earnest. Once a Blood horse has lost condition, particularly in winter, it seems to take an excessively long time for him to recuperate. As with most human beings, I had imagined it was easier to put weight on a horse than to take it off, but I learned differently. It began literally to hurt me when Be Fair did not look 'right', and thereafter I took great pains to prevent another decline, however small.

During late February, we spent another week at Alison's where she encouraged me by approving of Be Fair's condition and of the work I was giving him. David helped us every day with our dressage. As each lesson came to an end, he would ride him, searching for the extensions he was sure that Be Fair could produce.

Be Fair's natural pace was a short unspectacular one. He had only learnt to lower himself to the ground and stretch out to gallop properly at Punchestown, the previous year. His trot took longer to lengthen. He is an upright horse, short coupled, long legged and with a cocky high head and neck carriage. These, combined with his indomitable temperament, made it difficult for him to let go of himself and 'open up'. The sixth day of our week saw him finally receive and agree to understand David's message. He flung his fore-legs nearly horizontally out in front of him, maintaining a moment of suspension with each one. His hind-legs propelled him forwards as they snapped up high under his stomach, each one with similar momentary suspension. He never forgot the animation he felt at that moment of discovery. He must have known how magnificent he looked – he sensed the thrill onlookers felt as they watched his gleaming chestnut body pound across the arena, ears acutely pricked, tail swaying and bouncing with the exaggerated rhythm of his extended stride. Four years later, in front of thousands of spectators who crowded the banks bordering the Olympic arena as he turned up the centreline at the end of our test, instead of obeying the aid by striking off to canter, he could not resist bursting into extended trot.

After David had succeeded with him however, I had to suffer the familiar humiliation; Be Fair learnt very quickly that he did not have to trouble his hind-legs to do any work once I was riding. In his extended trot he flicked his toe out as far as he could in front of him and it felt marvellous. I imagined it looked it – David assured me that it did not – his hind-legs were not propelling him as they should. It took two more years before I even began to be able to produce the same suspension and supreme elegance that David could.

Cocktail parties and dances prior to events could be lonely affairs in those days. I was a junior and did not know many people. The reigning World and European Champion was Mary Gordon-Watson, and through her genuine and kind personality she frequently helped me to feel more at home. I remember being so thrilled the first time she spoke to me and rushed home to tell Be Fair that I had met Cornishman V's mother and that he really had to meet Cornishman himself one day. In a manner so unassuming that I do not believe she knew what she was doing, Mary would drop golden bits of information and advice into my lap. She gave me the tip about smearing the fronts of your horse's legs with Vaseline so that he would have a chance to slide rather than fall over a cross-country fence should he hit it. She also advised me not to do more than two events preparatory to Badminton. 'Corny only likes to do one now, he thinks he's so grand.'

By the time the Two Day Event at Crookham came about in mid-March, the fitness programme that Mexico Individual silver medallist Derek Allhusen had advised me to employ for Badminton, had reached the stage of twenty minutes slow cantering ending with either three-quarters of a mile or a mile gallop. The speed and endurance phase that year at Crookham plunged us straight into a mile of steeplechase followed by six kilometres of roads and tracks. Be Fair was becoming very nappy about starting and would rear and run backwards the moment I suggested that it was time to approach the flag. We discovered that if there were enough people behind him he could be persuaded to go up to the line. We knew this difficulty was not due to his unwillingness but to his nerves, which he had difficulty in controlling at the thought of the excitement which lay ahead. At every start thereafter he became each time a little worse.

On Crookham's dreary Phase C, winding through the repetitive heathland encompassing Tweseldown Racecourse, we became engrossed in watching the helter-skelter of some go-karts as we passed their race-track. My attention was abruptly caught by a voice.

'Hello there!' I looked ahead and saw a fellow competitor trotting towards us. He was also on Phase C, but he was going the right way. I swung Be Fair round and had to canter for some time to catch up on the time and distance lost through the go-karts distraction.

The cross-country was of Advanced standard and there were two particularly big fences over gaping ditches that frightened me enough to make me close my eyes as Be Fair galloped towards them. I felt that if he could negotiate that sort of obstacle then we would be one step nearer Badminton, and accordingly one step nearer he took me.

Preparations were going smoothly. We had suffered no setbacks of any kind and my confidence in Be Fair was as high after Crookham as it had been after Wylye – then in early April we went to Kinlet. We were advised that this was an ideal rehearsal for Badminton – big solid fences over a galloping course. When we arrived we found this to be true but we also found a very hilly course with a ground of soft, deep clay.

Be Fair was in with a chance after the dressage and the showjumping phases but then he rebelled across country. I am still not quite sure why he did. He arrived at the top of a bank leading down into the gully of the Water Garden fence, stopped and promptly reared and swung round in true 1969 style. I think he caught me complacently unawares again and maybe was offering me a reminder that he had not, and never would become a horse that could be switched onto 'automatic'. He made certain the judge gave him twenty penalties for a refusal, then tip-toed down through the crocus-lined bank and popped unconcerned across the stream and rail at the bottom. That evening during the long drive home against the rain my mother and I repeatedly analysed Be Fair's round across country. None of it had felt quite right. He seemed to be jumping without his normal zest, taking off over a fence and somehow only just managing to reach the other side to land. Why had he felt like this? Was it the soft going combined with the tiring hills that had robbed him of his habitual power-packed spring? We did not know, we could only surmise, and Badminton was a mere two weeks away.

The next day he was lame. The vet was exhorted to

come immediately for we could see no reason for the lameness in his near-fore. An able diagnostician, Mr Mahon, the vet, pressed his fore-finger into a spot on the muscles of Be Fair's inside fore-arm that produced a reaction as if he had stuck in a pin. We wondered if Be Fair had pulled a muscle when a pole was caught between his legs while practising in hock-deep mud in the collecting arena for the showjumping. Did that explain a little of the reason for his below-par performance across country we wondered. Ultrasonic treatment and five days of walking exercise erased the trouble: we decided to leave his entry in for Badminton and only withdraw if the going there was to be deep.

The day before we left for Badminton, although the ground was beginning to dry out, Be Fair still managed to churn up our local race-horse trainer, Toby Balding's precious gallops during his thirty minute canter. Thirty minutes of slow cantering interspersed with a half mile, half-speed gallop in the middle and a three-quarter mile, three-quarter-speed gallop at the end. A total distance covered of some nine miles without a pause. Be Fair seemed fitter than he had ever been.

The tack-room looked tidy by the time I had finished packing up for Badminton simply because there was nothing left in it to look untidy. I took everything with me, even the grooming machine just in case its vibratory effects were needed to calm Be Fair's nerves.

On the Monday morning we went for a final ride around the Hampshire lanes. I could not believe that in a few hours time we would be on the road heading for the place whose name alone evokes the principle ambition of nearly every event rider.

A mile from home Be Fair started to slow his walk. He put his nose high in the air and curled his upper lip to show his teeth. A small girl walking with her mother down the road pointed at him and squealed 'Isn't he funny, he's laughing . . .' He was not being funny at all.

Something was very definitely wrong. He slowed up more and I jumped off. Gently and with several pauses I coaxed him home. I had little idea why he should have it but I suspected he was suffering from acute tummy-ache or colic. Hopes of taking on our first Badminton faded fast.

Later that morning the vet arrived with his usual swirl of gravel to find my father and I struggling to pour a drench down Be Fair's throat. His head was strung up to a beam by a lunge rein, which my father held tightly, so that his nose pointed towards the ceiling. Meanwhile, I balanced on the stable door, my head precariously near a light-bulb, trying to deliver the medicine. The vet concluded that I must have fed him too many of the high protein tic-beans that for the past fortnight he had been eating to increase his energy. He was not given another bean; the tummy-ache subsided and we were able to set off to Badminton the following day.

Turning off the motorway into the small winding roads of Gloucestershire was in itself an excitement. The countryside was dramatically different from Hampshire. The sand-coloured stone is everywhere, in walls and farmyards, small cottages and large houses. The two miles of narrow lane that leads into the tiny village of Badminton had already been roped by the police on either side, to prevent illicit parking. My heart started to beat faster and Be Fair knew something was up. Maybe he felt the box slow down a little and, stretching his head down low over the chest partition, he peered from behind my seat through the windscreen. A Union Jack flying at the top of a flag-pole came into view and then the greenish, turreted copper roof of the great house could be seen above the trees. I could not wait to arrive. I put my foot down and Be Fair was jerked to the back of his stall. He refastened his seat-belt and did not risk another look.

I drove to where I remembered the main stable-yard

to be. The lay-out of Badminton was not foreign as I had soaked it all in that July when we had come to practise in the lake. I had told Be Fair of the beautiful interior stables that he would be living in, with their shining brass doorhandles and rack-rings and newly painted wood. The stable manager asked my name and ran a finger down his list.

'You will have to turn round, Miss, and go back up the hill and left-handed down to the Portcullis yard. That's where your horse is stabled.'

Slightly disappointed at not being in the main yard, I turned the box around and went to find this Portcullis yard, which I imagined would be just as exquisite. It was not. It was an old farmyard of perhaps fifteen stables, most of whose grey doors had the paint peeling off. It was scruffy and in sharp contrast to the new white shavings which came tumbling out of each stable as its door was opened. I had wanted Be Fair bedded on shavings and that was why, I discovered later, he could not be in the main yard which was only for straw bedding.

Be Fair obviously loved his new home and quickly became well contented. The peace and quiet of this yard was worth double the paint and shining brass of the other. Here, the public rarely discovered us; instead they shuffled in a constant stream down the corridors of the main stables, peering into some of them by lifting a blanket forming a mock curtain and knocking off the 'Do Not Disturb' notices that an irritated groom or rider had erected in an effort to give their horse some rest. In the Portcullis yard the doors were divided and the horses could look out and inhale the crisp Badminton air.

I could not wait to take Be Fair for a ride in the park. I began to brush out all the tacky new shavings that he had covered himself in while rolling before I had even time to take off his best navy-blue day rug. I would brush the rug out later, I thought, because that would take even longer than the horse.

Oliver Plum was no less delighted with his new surroundings than Be Fair and I. He stalked through the great iron gates which led into the park ten yards in front of us, and confronted a Land Rover as it shrieked to a halt. The window snapped open and a felt hat and glasses appeared in the aperture.

'Put that b . . . thing on a lead. There are deer in this park and the Duke of Beaufort does not want them disturbed.'

That, I imagined, was Lieutenant-Colonel Frank Weldon, the power behind the throne of the Badminton Horse Trials. I had never met him before and no one had ever introduced him to me. I spent quite a long time enjoying a feeling of anonymity as I was sure he had no idea of my name. I soon learnt, however, that very little slipped his notice.

The following day Wanna arrived to look after Be Fair for me over the competition. Most of the competitors attended the briefing in the Village Hall that morning. The technicalities were explained by Colonel Weldon with some additional extra-dry humour to encourage us. He then headed a train of over twenty-five Land Rovers on the drive round the roads and tracks, Phases A and C, stopping for half an hour to allow us to walk the kidney-shaped steeplechase course. There is always a battle for the first few places behind Colonel Weldon's Land Rover. I was in Mike Tucker's Land Rover and although he lost the initial struggle to gain pride of place as we started on Phase C, he came with a late run, skidding and sliding up the steep hill which begins Worcester Avenue. We arrived crabwise at the top of the hill and straightened out into first position to be greeted by a view, a mile down the avenue, of the beautiful early eighteenth-century grey stone house, gazing regally towards us across the glistening lake. The excitement of driving the roads and tracks fairly set the pace for the whole competition. Like everyone must do, I felt at sea during my first Badminton and was nagged by incessant doubts. Was Be Fair fit enough? Had I remembered the way on the roads and tracks? Would I forget the dressage test in the numbness of the moment? Should I really be at Badminton at all?

It always amazed me how willing any of the top competitors were to offer advice. I was not sure how much work I should give Be Fair between the Wednesday and the Saturday's cross-country to keep him physically in tune. I asked Richard Walker, who was always generous with his help. He modestly suggested that he found it best to give his horse a good gallop on the Thursday in order to make him breathe deeply and to clear his lungs thoroughly.

'Then on the Friday,' he suggested, 'a short sharp sprint just to keep his wind clear. You want him to pull up quite unstrained, feeling on top of the world.' In my imagination I could see Be Fair pulling up and patting his chest and saying that he was now quite ready to face anything in the world. It was helpful advice and the simile he used boosted my morale through my imagination.

First of all, however, we had to negotiate the dressage phase. When Richard Meade and Poacher had won Badminton in 1970, I remember watching the Borwicks' daughter, Tessa, doing her test and then finding that she had to withdraw the following day because the horse was not quite sound. Because I knew Tessa and had been able to put myself in her position, I remember being overcome by imagining riding in that seemingly huge and grand arena. I had felt that the thrill of managing to reach even that elevation must make up a little for the disappointment of being unable to continue the competition.

Two years later, after no less than three and a half hours of working in, I was in that grand arena in the flesh, not in my imagination, and with me was the 'town horse' from the Reform School.

As we were of little consequence we performed our test on the afternoon of the first day of dressage, when most of the spectators had not yet arrived. This was fortunate, because without top-hat and tails I might have looked out of place the following day and also the lack of crowd distraction was helpful to both our nerves. Nonetheless the sense of the occasion was very apparent. Be Fair kept himself just below boiling point and a reasonable test left us in twelfth place at the end of the two days – twenty-four points behind Mark Phillips and Great Ovation who, with fifty-nine penalties, led for the second year running.

That evening, Mark kindly agreed to walk the cross-country Phase D with me. I had been given much helpful counsel, both from Lady Hugh and from Dick Stillwell, and now I felt I needed the loose ends tying up by someone who was accustomed to actually riding the course. Maybe I had walked the course twice previously with a shock-absorber round my head, or maybe it was because Friday evening is that much nearer to Saturday's cross-country than Thursday morning. Whichever it was, that

Badminton, 1972: Our dressage was almost reasonable (*Clive Hiles*)

final walk round with Mark and his father really tensed me up. Those boughs used to build the fences seemed increasingly unforgiving. They required more than respect, they required skilled riding and bold jumping. Oh help! What was I doing here? The great Dumbell jump loomed up at the top of the gentle rise from the Lake.

'If I ever make it this far, should I take the maximum height and spread (3′11″ x 6′7″) of the direct route, or should I pull up and fiddle down the escape chute?' I asked.

'Kick on, kick on,' was all Mark could say. 'If you have got this far you'll be all right to kick on over that . . .' Every time I tried to muddle myself by finding a reason to go the most awkward way or tried to discuss the technicalities, Mark would simply reply, 'Just kick on.'

The three of us walked in silence from the last fence, the Whitbread Bar, and as we did so, I felt something warm running down the back of my throat. I had not had a nose-bleed for months. When I do have one it is normally attributed to pressure, caused by a weather change or, it seems, by walking Badminton's cross-country course. It was a streaming nose-bleed and I did not have a handkerchief. I borrowed one from Mark's father, Colonel Phillips, and spent a few minutes thanking them for their help, and convincing them that I was fine and that my nose-bleed was quite normal.

When you are feeling sick with emotion, it has the effect of slowing you up; leaden legs seem to refuse to transport you anywhere at speed. It was this feeling that I had as I tottered back to see Be Fair. I sorted my nose out before I arrived because I knew he would be worried if he saw or smelt the blood. The stables were quiet. Wanna, his temporary nanny, had gone with the others, either to supper or to take a look at the course herself. I let myself into Be Fair's box. He was standing with his bottom in the corner, resting, a slightly disgruntled look on his face. He had already finished the tiny ration of hay that he was allowed before cross-country day. I put his head on my shoulder, my arms round his neck and began to tell him the course. The more I talked to him the more I felt the confidence that had drained away returning little by little with every fence that we jumped in our imagination. By the Whitbread Bar I squeezed him tight in a big hug, 'We've done it,' I said and then I realised, 'Oh, no – we haven't . . . not yet. *Can* you do it Be Fair? I know *you* can, but can you do it for *me*? I am certain to make mistakes – all the way round – will you be able to do it in spite of these?'

That evening, driving back to Wickwar where my parents and I were staying, my car rattled over a cattle-grid at the edge of some common land, and frightened two magpies into flight. I went into my mother's bedroom and found her changing for a late dinner. 'How did your course walk go? Did Mark help you?' she asked.

'I don't really know. I had hoped to tie up lots of loose ends with his advice, but I never got any – he just kept on saying "kick on".'

She thought, and then replied, 'I should think it was the best thing he could have said to you at this point.' She was right – again. I had been tying myself in knots over technicalities and was beginning to forget the most important thing of all: to go out onto that course and *ride*.

These thoughts ran continuously through my mind the next day as Be Fair and I made steady progress down Phase C. I knew that I would have a few time penalties on the steeplechase because I had mistimed it – remembering the rocket I had been given at Punchestown, I had now erred on the opposite side. Determined not to sap more of Be Fair's energy than I need, I had tried to time it too accurately and did not appreciate how quickly six seconds disappeared. We had collected 4.8 penalties. It did not seriously worry me but it niggled me and deepened my concentration for the test ahead.

On Phase C we cantered steadily up the rise at the beginning of Worcester Avenue which still showed the skid marks of Wednesday's Land Rover race. In the distance was Badminton House but the water was no longer visible in front of it, only a dark mass of what was presumably people, gathered round the Lake fences. I felt new life surge into Be Fair; he knew where he was because he had used the avenue for our gallops. He became quite strong and wanted to go faster. I was glad for he had begun to feel rather dull. As we neared the end of the avenue I picked up the booming of the loudspeaker following the progress of a competitor as he wended his way from one challenging fence to the next. My stop-watch told me that we were ahead of time as we entered the park. I remembered the tips in Sheila Willcox's book, *The Event Horse*,* and pulled Be Fair back to a walk. There was a shrill whistle as the mounted steward warned of the imminent approach on the cross-country course of the next competitor. For a few seconds I watched as the horse and rider trickled up the ramp to the edge of the massive Ski-jump, dropped down, jumped the Triple-bar at its base and, a hundred yards further on, pitched onto the Normandy Bank and sprang cleanly off again.

Be Fair jiggled and jogged, his telescopic neck held high as he looked about him at the crowd and the cars. Children screamed when they saw him coming and ran for their mothers. He was not in the least bit interested in watching the other horse jump, only in counting up how many people were there to watch him. As he neared the Lake, although we were a 100 yards from the finish of Phase C, I nearly lost the way. Rows of cars were parked between us and the finish and I had to canter in order to find my way round them and arrive in the box

*Pelham Books, 1973

on time. There was a low-toned gasp from the mass of spectators who had been drawn to the water, like sun-baked camels to an oasis.

'Cor! That rider must have fallen into the water. Woopee! Let's go and have a look,' screamed one little boy to his friend and they belted towards the Lake grasping their candy floss. 'What a pity,' I thought, 'that competitor was going so well at the three fences I saw him over – he quite warmed my heart because he made it all look possible.'

The ten minute break in the box is another of the bitter-sweet characteristics of the Three Day Event. On the one hand it is lovely to hand your sweating, blowing horse over to a team such as the General (my father), his Lady (my mother) and Wanna, who even in those early days, made a skilled and quick job of unsaddling, washing down and checking bandages and studs. On the other hand, you are a bit weary. You have no alternative but to sit on the grass or on the loo for eight whole minutes. There, to realise that the apprehension you had always felt for others as you watched them start, was striking you, in quadruple form, because suddenly it was apprehension for your horse and yourself. It was you who was about to start on that huge cross-country course.

'*Smile* – you do it for *fun* don't forget.' My mother's cheerful voice interrupted my thoughts. She had seen my pensive face, whitening by the minute.

How true. Why else did I do it if it was not for fun? With difficulty, my father legged me up onto a restless Be Fair, two minutes before the steward was due to start us, and he led us once round the box. As my father enticed Be Fair to the line the man began to count us down.

'10, 9, 8, 7, 6 . . .'
'Don't forget you've got legs – use them – *kick*!'
'3, 2 . . .'
'And don't forget you do it for fun.'

'GO!'

My father's last two morsels of encouragement rang through the air after me as we galloped towards the first fence. Be Fair jumped it well, but after that I forgot about my legs. The fourth fence was a big blind drop amongst the trees in Huntsman's Close, followed by a sharp right-hand turn over some rails. It was here that we had once watched the television with interest to see Fair and Square. But we had seen him break down on landing over the Leap. He had been unable to rise high enough for the following rails and gave himself and Sheila a crashing fall. That was 1969. Three years later his son made mince-meat of exactly the same complex.

Nevertheless the message demanding more impetus frequently failed to reach from my brain all the way down to my heels in time. The signal would stop short somewhere around my waist. Invariably my arms had to hastily intercept the order and take out my whip to produce the required impulsion in time. This happened many times, particularly at a fence which frightened me.

The first belt that Be Fair had was after Huntsman's Close, at the Elephant Trap, whose gargantuan ditch had left me feeling cold when I walked the course. We

Badminton, 1972: Fence four, a big blind drop amongst the trees in Huntsman's Close (*Clive Hiles*)

steadied considerably for the Quarry: he jumped carefully but boldly over the small stone wall, which stood at the brink of its vertical side, and dropped neatly into the pit below.

The steward blew his shrill whistle to clear the crowds as the Keeper's rails loomed up and Be Fair received another wallop – it was another huge ditch. This time it had a single telegraph pole across it, reminiscent of the Trakhener at Tidworth but very definitely its great-grandfather. The Ski-jump, the Normandy Bank and the Lake were ahead, the three fences that worried me most and they were all one after the other. I started to feel tired and floppy and yet I was not even half the way round. 'You're not tired, you can't be. What have you been skipping for five whole weeks for? Why has Be Fair worked so hard to get fit? Come on girl, pull yourself together.' My school teachers would have been amazed, their reports always stated that I lacked self-control.

The whistle sounded again. Summoning my strength I hooked Be Fair back to a bouncy canter and then to a trot. I held him tightly together between my hands and

Fence fourteen, the Ski-jump, followed two strides later by . . .

legs. We turned the sharp corner and jogged up the ramp to the edge of the Ski-jump. From the summit we could survey most of Badminton Park through the oak branches. 'That's not why we're here though, Be Fair.' Just this once I did remember to kick. I felt his body lowering like a cat as he sprang gently off the edge, landed in perfect balance on the sharp slope and two strides later, effortlessly jumped the Triple Bar. No one had ever told him not to hurtle off the edge of ramps and land with a heavy thud yards further down like most horses will at their first attempt – he just knew how to do it because he is highly intelligent, he is bold and he is trusting.

Fear made me forget my legs again as I approached the Normandy Bank and he squirmed onto the grassed top with virtually no impulsion left. Amazingly he found something extra and gathering himself together he sprang over the rails and down the six foot drop off the bank. As he landed I patted him and smiled with unutterable relief. The previous year I had watched Eddie Boylan's horse break its spine jumping the Normandy Bank, that

... the Triple Bar (*Clive Hiles*)

year in the opposite direction. The horse had landed badly and had rolled awkwardly and fatally back into the ditch.

The television was beamed in on us then for the first time in our lives. Erna, our cook, was at home, sitting on the edge of her seat as she watched. She could not believe that she was seeing Be Fair and me on television. For the whole of the following week, as she stored up mounds of extra apple and carrot peelings, she could not stop repeating all that Raymond Brooks-Ward, the commentator, had said:

'One of our up-and-coming combinations this. Eighteen-year-old Lucinda Prior-Palmer with Be Fair, her beautiful nine-year-old chestnut whom she has ridden since their Pony Club days. She's always smiling this one, they really seem to love doing the cross-country.' It was true that as each terror was left behind, there were a few seconds of smiling relief and patting before the memory of what was to come clouded the joy.

Nothing could stop Erna recapturing those moments as she repeatedly imitated the BBC, 'And now here we have Number 43 coming into the Lake fence. There has been a lot of trouble here at the Lake today, a lot of wet breeches ... and Be Fair's *in* and ... out again ... and they're off like a bomb.' That was the bit Erna really liked and remembered for months. With her German accent she would mimic 'off like a bomb,' whenever it was remotely applicable. She even screeched it in the kitchen one day as a spider ran across the sink and down the plug-hole.

The dreaded Dumb-bell responded well to the attitude Mark had advised as did the Vicarage Ditch and the first Luckington Lane Crossing. Gradually I began to slip into a trance which even the warning screech of the whistle failed to break. 'Have we really got this far – is it possible?' I felt a tiny bit faint; I could not believe that we were both ourselves, that we were both here three-quarters of our way round our first Badminton. In this haze we approached Tom Smith's. Two large stone walls at right angles to each other, to be negotiated without turning a circle or leaving the surrounding penalty area. Everything went wrong at once and so quickly that it took some time to analyse what in fact had happened. Certainly I had not collected Be Fair enough before I jumped part A, but as I tried to turn sharp right on landing to face up to part B, Be Fair kept going in a straight line running down the second wall. The reins had slipped unhindered through my right hand. Later on someone did remark that I should not wear leather gloves, for they slip hopelessly when they become wet with the horse's sweat. All the pent-up emotions and anxieties finally burst and left me with a feeling of hopelessness and defeat. We were so nearly home and then I had to make a silly mistake like that incurring twenty penalties. I felt such a fool.

Be Fair nearly fell at the next fence, a double of hedges back across Luckington Lane. That gave me a fright sufficient to pull me together and I remembered to write in my little book of words under 'M' for mistakes, 'If you make a mistake don't let that awful feeling of despair and panic overcome you; it is then that you'll make another one and it might be even worse. *You owe it to our horse* to ride the rest of the course as coolly and as

Dwarfed by the Vicarage Ditch (*Findlay Davidson*)

positively as you can. NB Bad '72 – Luckington Lane, having run out at preceding Tom Smith's Walls.'

I did not hurry Be Fair down the final stretch of mown grass directly in front of the house. I had forgotten the Tom Smith's Walls incident and was instead already beginning to slow him up as I filled with elation. 'We've nearly done it, Be Fair' I panted. 'We've nearly got round Badminton, but mustn't forget – last-fence-itis.' Last year at Tidworth I had nearly up-ended through riding with the reckless abandon that the last fence tempts. Be Fair jumped the Whitbread Bar with the care and power with which he had jumped the first. He was well within himself and not feeling in the least tired. I was jubilant. Because I was so grateful to him I did not see why he should canter further than he need. I pulled up and we trotted gently and joyously through the finish. (Those few wasted seconds proved expensive, each one costs 0.4 of a penalty, and in the final result we finished 0.3 behind Debbie West and Baccarat.)

None of us could really believe that it was true. We fell about hugging Be Fair and each other, no doubt maddening other competitors in the box by being in their way. We re-lived each fence together. Mummy and Daddy had seen us over nearly half the course on the closed circuit television; they wanted to know what it had felt like. Equally I wanted to know what it had looked like. I turned round looking for my real live Badminton horse but he was already on his way back to the stables with Wanna, who wanted to wash him down and make him comfortable as soon as possible. I wanted to be with him to thank him and praise him so I ran after him and Wanna and accompanied them back to our cosy little yard. My parents followed and as we rubbed Be Fair dry and pasted his legs with some comforting clay, the re-enactment continued. It was then that we noticed the Vaseline on the reins and realised that my mother had greased his legs in the box and must then have grabbed the reins in order to hold Be Fair still while I was legged-up. We presumed that this had not aided my attempt to make the sharp turn for part B of Tom Smith's walls.

Later in the afternoon we wandered up to the arena to where the score-boards were sighted. I was still in a daze of disbelief. My crash-hat and pale yellow silk were still on my head; my number still covered the yellow jersey that I wore. The first thing we saw as we neared the board was my older brother running towards us, gangly legs and arms waving in every direction.

'Christ!' he yelled. 'You're lying seventh. How the hell? I didn't think you were meant to get round.'

None of us had expected to see Simon. He was not in the least concerned with horses and competitions and never came to watch. The most interest he ever took was in trying to annoy me by asking me on my return from an outing, 'Did you win? Why not?' At the beginning I did fall into the trap and rose sharply to the bait by preaching him my creed of, 'I believe in competing to do your best and to have fun, not to win, win, win . . .' He had, however, heard of Badminton before I happened to be riding there and as he was staying with friends in Gloucestershire he had been unable to resist sneaking over at the end of the day to see what had befallen me.

Karol, my ever-enthusiastic half-sister, left her children at home and the following afternoon she and Simon sat together in the stands and worked each other up into a frenzied state of excitement as they watched the final phase, the showjumping.

Jumping in the accustomed reverse order of merit, I had plenty of time to watch how the course rode. Be Fair never showjumped with much suppleness and he was no less stiff than usual that day. All the same he managed a clear round despite my seeing several of my wretched 'long ones'. He was becoming used to being flattened out over a jump and generally managed to pull his feet out of the way of the poles. Such methods tend towards rather too many anxious moments, however. The next two competitors in the ring after Be Fair each knocked one fence down. These mistakes were greeted with an uncontrollable cheer from two particular people in the stands, who realised that those errors put Be Fair two places higher. The two particular people were sitting next to a great family friend, who eventually had to tell them both to shut up. Neither of them had yet been so animated by their sister's 'horse-stuff' and they were enjoying their self-indulgence as they egged each other on.

Be Fair ended his first Badminton in fifth place. In the final line-up, the Queen came into the arena to present the prizes. She gave Be Fair his rosette and asked where he had come from. 'Birmingham, ma'am,' was the reply.

I drove Be Fair home alone with Oliver Plum that evening. I was glad – I did not want other company. As we left behind us the unmatched magic of the Gloucestershire countryside and joined the mechanical bustle of the M4, I switched on the radio. The 6.30 news told me that Mark Phillips had just won Badminton for the second year running, beating Richard Meade by the fraction of a time fault that he had incurred in the showjumping phase. I repeated it to myself and then out loud to Be Fair, and then it hit me. 'Be Fair, it's true, you and I were there too. You and I also competed and completed and were fifth.' As I turned off the M4 onto a quieter road I switched off the radio and my mind flooded with memories of all we had been through together: the problem horse who would never suit a teenager, the ditch at that first Pony Club hunter trials, the amount of times I had fallen off, that four hour session in Alison's covered school. He and I were alone now. I hated to be seen crying, but with Be Fair I felt I could because he was the only one who would truly understand how I felt at that moment.

The next day I withdrew Be Fair from Tidworth.

6 A Shaft of Light

The telephone was quieter in those days. It rang eight days after Badminton at the unusual time of 10.15 am.

'Bet that's them ringing up to tell you that you're on the Olympic team short-list,' joked my brother as he wandered upstairs. I was sitting in the kitchen poring over some photographs of Badminton that had arrived with the morning's post.

'Oh shut up, of course they won't put us on it . . . we're, I mean, I'm too young.' I returned.

Someone had picked up the telephone upstairs, my mother I presumed. My insides did turn over as Simon's words went through my mind, but I have a defence mechanism against disappointment which has been in operation for several years. I pad myself out against failure by not allowing myself any wild delusions in the first place. My insides turned back the other way and I continued to gloat over the photographs. A few minutes later I heard an irregular thundering of feet bounding down the stairs accompanied by a bellow from Simon, 'It was! It was! It was Martin Whitely on the telephone asking you and Be Fair to join the short-list.' Breathless he burst into the kitchen.

'Will you kindly shut up?' I was eighteen and I was not going to be kidded any longer by my twenty-one-year-old brother.

'I promise you, I'm not being funny, it was Martin Whitely and he did ask you to join the short-list for the Olympic Games – go and ask Mum.'

I was loathe to rise from the table to go and ask Mum. Convinced that he was trying to pull my leg, I had no intention of giving him the satisfaction of succeeding.

Instead I told him that it was a ridiculously unsubtle joke. How could he expect me to believe him, when only minutes before he had said facetiously that the telephone call must be from the head of the selection committee.

He won in the end and I went slowly and reluctantly out of the kitchen and up the stairs. As soon as I was out of his earshot I stormed across the top floor and burst into Mum's bedroom.

'Is it true – was that Martin Whitely?'

It was true.

I rushed out to the field to interrupt Be Fair's holiday and tell him. He was too interested in the small sweet shoots of spring grass and would not be caught. I had to explain from a distance that he was one of the five possibles for the Munich Games. I also had to explain that there were five probables on the short-list as well.

The following week I had to attend a meeting held for the ten on the short-list. The committee, as well as Peter Scott-Dunn, the team vet, sat round Martin Whitely's highly polished dining-room table and saw each one of us individually accompanied by our various trainers. I went by myself because so many people had helped train me that I could not think which one to ask to come. Walking into that dining-room was rather worse than going into the Head Sister's study at my convent school.

These influential gentlemen turned out to be kind and good humoured and advised me of the programme Be Fair ought to follow in order to be Three Day Event fit for the team trial at Eridge, an important Two Day Event in August, three weeks prior to the Olympics.

As I drove home I remembered the girl at Alison's who only a year ago had warned me of the unfriendliness and unhelpfulness of those at the top. I wondered where she had found such a story.

Life was taking on a very new look.

The local paper arrived and took some lovely photographs of Be Fair. Southern Television came next to try to interview me while I held him. Be Fair did not mind ordinary cameras but television was as strange to him as it was to me and I had to put him back in his stable and brave it alone. I remember being hopeless. I had always loved acting on the stage at school and therefore I had not thought television would be any problem. Instead I found my voice quavered and my shoes seemed to grow larger the more I stared at them. It was a cold-blooded situation, I thought, acting to a piece of whirring machinery. It took longer than that initial effort to realise that firstly, you do not act, and secondly there is no reason to be afraid.

The great Cornishman V, a 'probable' on the short-list and holder of three gold medals, asked Be Fair, four years his junior, to stay during June. They wanted to enjoy each other's company for a week during the early and rather dull fitness work.

The four of us went on long and beautiful rides climbing the hot and still Dorset Downs every day. It was far from dull. Once we took Mary's two greyhounds with us and had our own hunt as they put up a hare and coursed it round in a large circle bounding through the tall wisping grass. Corny and Be Fair galloped alongside each other in pursuit. Every now and again Be Fair would veer sharply sideways to avoid one of Corny's enormous fly-bucks. He had not bucked himself since his early days at the riding school; I hoped that he would not be reminded.

He came home and swanked about his stay with 'his friend' to a small angular bay gelding, Wide Awake, who stood in the stable opposite on the other side of the tack-room. Be Fair never liked Wide Awake very much; he was the first serious intruder on his territory. His owner, Mrs Vicki Phillips, had been searching for someone to ride him when she saw us on television at Badminton. I was able to tell Be Fair that he ought not to blame me for someone else being in his home – it was all his fault for going so well at Badminton.

It was quite early in the morning and Alison Oliver thought she must have had a worse night than she had realised. She drew her curtains back, and looked out of her window to see, riding round the field, an apparition in bright pink jeans, black tail-coat and top-hat with shoulder length hair flying out from under it. I was staying at Alison's for a week and David had suggested that I had a trial run in this fancy dress, which had been borrowed to wear at the forthcoming Rothmans Dressage Championship at the Royal International Horse Show in July. Some horses are frightened by the flapping of a tail-coat on their sides. Some riders' heads wobble so badly that their top-hat is shaken off. I still find great difficulty in not resembling one of those loose-necked plastic dogs which dangle in the rear windows of cars and madden you if you are behind it in a slow moving traffic-jam.

Be Fair was going well during our week's stay at Alison's and it was disappointing that the occasion of the Championships at Syon Park was too much for him – he misbehaved thoroughly. Our score was a long way behind those of the others on the short-list.

Shortly before Eridge, Be Fair rolled on a stone during his daily half-an-hour in the field and cut the side of his wither exactly where the saddle fits. I could not do any dressage or canter work. Instead I went for long rides bareback to keep him ticking over. During one of these I lost Oliver Plum. I called and called as I searched the wood and the hedgerows for over an hour. Eventually he appeared, smirking, from some undergrowth that bordered a quiet country lane. I was furious with him at his disobedience. I jumped off Be Fair, took the reins over his head and began to teach Oliver a lesson with my stick. Be Fair took fright, yanked backwards and the reins shot from my hand. Feeling that he was free, he swung round and trotted away down the lane through the shadows of the bordering trees. I made a lunge for his tail recalling the story of Jane Bullen tripping over as she ran alongside Our Nobby on Phase C in Mexico. She caught Nobby by the tail but I did not catch Be Fair.

My 'possible Olympic horse' broke into a canter and clattered out of sight round a blind corner. I thought for a moment, glaring at Oliver with temporary hatred. Then I ran down the lane too, not because I expected to catch him, but because I could not think of anything better to do. A few hundred yards from the corner he was standing motionless, chewing at the moss-covered banks of the lane. I went quietly up to him talking all the time as naturally as possible, hoping that he would not realise how terrified I was of the consequences should I fail to catch him. He did not move, he could not. He was stepping on the buckle of his reins and that was the only reason he had ever stopped.

I cursed Oliver for being the cause of such a near disaster and then realised that I was cursing the trees, Oliver was not with me. Be Fair and I went back down the lane to look for him. We found him still sitting in his place of punishment. That was one of the rare occasions he stayed where he was put – except I never remembered actually telling him to sit there.

At Eridge in early August, the short-list was stabled together in a farmyard in Eridge Park, half a mile from the start of the hard-baked, clay track of the cross-country course. Peter Scott-Dunn vetted all the horses the evening prior to the competition and was amazed that he still had ten out of ten sound horses. Before the last Olympics most of the short-list had disintegrated and they had had to do some last minute match-making between different horses and riders in order to send a team at all. Although it reduced my chances to almost nil

I was glad that there was still a 'full house' left. I had worried all summer that if they hit a catastrophe similar to the one prior to Mexico, they would ask if, for the country's honour, they could take Be Fair away from me and put someone better on him. I kept thinking that it would probably be Richard Walker. I liked him and admired his quiet horsemanship. I could not decide whether or not I would be noble. Fortunately I never had to make up my mind.

After we had completed the dressage and show-jumping phases, the selectors decided that six of the short-list would not do the steeplechase phase as the ground was too hard to risk it. The remaining four on the short-list were allowed to continue in the competition in its entirety.

It was a sensible decision but had a disastrous effect. Mark and Great Ovation fell in the water, Janet and Larkspur had a stop and Richard Meade had a fall with both the horses he was riding – Wayfarer and Lauriston.

The Americans, en route for Munich, were also using Eridge as their final selection trial. They too had an unpleasant dress-rehearsal having missed Phase B for the same reason. Be Fair finished the competition proper in fourth place after an excellent cross-country, despite us nearly missing a fence because my attention was distracted by a man on a horse trotting down Phase C. He wore a pair of brightly coloured knickers patterned with stars and stripes and the next best thing to no breeches at all – a very thin pair of transparent nylon ones. I saw him later looking even more indecent as he had had a similar experience to Mark and fell into the water. I realised that he was the American, Mike Plumb, veteran of international Three Day Events. In my opinion he shares today with Richard Meade the title of the world's best Three Day Event competitor – but Richard does not share Mike's weight problem.

Sometime after we had finished the cross-country,

Lars Sederholm came up to me and congratulated me on how well Be Fair had gone both at Eridge and at Badminton earlier in the year.

'I never would beleeeve it, Luzinda,' he said in his excellent Swedish-accented English. 'I went to look at Be Fair for a client to buy when he was advertised in *Horse and Hound* in 1968. He would not leave the stable-yard – he just reared and reared.' Lars is a highly critical man but he can compliment when he feels it is right. Several times over the last few years, he has inconspicuously criticised or encouraged me – always much to my advantage. In retrospect, what he said at Eridge was high praise. At the time I was not thinking about compliments, I only thought how strange it was that Be Fair would not leave his stableyard for others who had come to see him, and yet the day we came he was as willing as an angel. I still think it strange. I believe he knew something through that Extra Sensory Perception of his – I believe he knew that our futures would be inextricably entwined.

Undaunted by the pile-ups their chosen few had experienced, the selectors named their six for the Olympics. I surprised myself by finding that I actually shed a tear when I learnt that I was not to go to Munich. All along I knew that we were the tenth of the ten on the short-list and would only go if serious trouble befell five others in a row. Yet something must have built up in my subconscious which burst into the open when the last thread of hope was finally cut. I spoke to myself seriously, thinking that the defence mechanism must be slipping. I realised that we had done very little to prove ourselves in comparison to the others. I started to wonder if we would ever be in such a position again or whether this was our first and last glimpse of the top. I recalled an article that had appeared in *The Times* after Badminton. The reporter thought that we had produced one of the most notable performances of the competition and would surely be a force to be reckoned with in the future. That had stuck in my mind and given me hope, but I now wondered if those words would prove to have any truth behind them in the end.

The cream were involved in the Olympic Games which left the milk a welcome gap to trickle through for the remainder of the autumn season.

Be Fair swept off with the Open Intermediate class at Stocklands in mid-August although we were lucky not to take a ducking. It was the only time he had to jump a fence whose take-off and landing were both in water. As usual he was busy at play, making the biggest splash his front legs could produce as he trotted the fifty yards through the lake. He was so enjoying himself sending up spray that he never appeared to see the telegraph pole erected in the middle of the water. Somehow he struggled across in a series of jerks.

The day after Stocklands we took Be Fair back to his old reform school. Mrs Firth was having him to stay as a non-paying guest for the week, while we went to support the side in the Olympic Games.

Open Intermediate, Stocklands, 1972. 'We were lucky not to take a ducking' (*Clive Hiles*)

'My privilege,' she said, 'to have his Lordship to stay – though I would have paid you to take him away three years ago.' She no longer referred to him as 'the town horse'.

Our family are inclined to be doers, not watchers. Nonetheless we had decided to borrow a caravan and go to Munich. It would probably be our only chance to go to the Olympic Games, for this time they were comparatively near to England. Obviously there was the added incentive of having been involved to an extent ourselves, and we had come to know the team and its trappings quite well.

We had a bird's-eye view of the dressage as we sat in a huge semi-circular stand whose capacity was 50,000. The stand was shaded by a hanging roof without one single upright to support it. Feelings similar to those I had known when I watched Tessa Borwick do her test at Badminton two years earlier, went through me now, only this time the feeling was more mature, the imagination a little more realistic. Mary and Richard made a superbly subtle and tactful job of the dressage on a Corny and a Lauriston quite electrified by the atmosphere. The thought that I did not have to take Be Fair in there filled me with relief. I would not have known how to cope with the tense excitability Be Fair would have felt in the vastness of that Riem stadium.

It was thrilling to watch our team blast their way through the cross-country, narrowly overhauling the Americans at the end of the day. Richard Meade rode Derek Allhusen's young and inexperienced Lauriston through the combination fence, Number 23, without a false step and was the only rider all day who cleared it through sheer good riding and not through luck. My admiration for such skill increased.

It is history now that Great Britain won two Gold Medals for the Three Day Event in Munich. It was sensational and thrilling, yet inexplicably it lacked something. I do not know what it was – Badminton has it – any other event in the world that I have witnessed does not.

Munich-inspired confidence was brimming as we set off late in August for the easternmost point of Kent to the Knowlton Horse Trials. I wanted to fly to Ireland the following week to look at a four year old I might try to buy and I wanted to win the Advanced class in order to pay my return fare.

One hundred and twenty miles still lay ahead of us when we were enveloped in clouds of foul smelling smoke as my mother and I drove up the M3. The fan-belt had broken. We arrived at Knowlton very much later than we intended that afternoon and quickly walked a rock-hard cross-country course. Oliver Fox-Pitt, the organiser and an event rider himself, was already on his tractor beginning to rotovate the baked clay course. The timing was immaculate: as Oliver drove the tractor up the final hill on the course an ominous rumble in the sky spelt rain. Most of that night boomed with an electric storm as the continuous rain made a soup of the cross-country course.

The next morning I left the ramp down for Be Fair to study his new surroundings while I went to walk the course again. When I was at the furthest point the clouds took a deep breath and started their production all over again. I finished the walk and returned to the box, where I found most of my riding clothes already soaking and water in the bottom of each of my leather boots. Be Fair, still dry, regarded me without enthusiasm as I struggled into wet breeches and coat.

Momentarily cheered by a very useful dressage and showjumping, I added to the discomforts of the English climate by throwing it all away in the cross-country through forgetting to kick – again. We sloshed to a halt in front of yet another corner fence. When the going is that holding, it is wise to remember to use double the leg power and change into four wheel drive. We discovered that it was even more important to ride Be Fair in this manner, for he did not seem to relish the deep as he did the hard. His long legs and short body presumably were not designed for such conditions and he produced a void feeling of powerlessness similar to that he had given me at Kinlet in the spring.

The Burghley Three Day Event in mid-September was a fortnight later and was fortunately 'on top of the ground'. Be Fair made light work of the cross-country. There was, however, one of the hated corner fences, forming part of the penultimate combination. All through Phase C I had prayed that someone would approach me in the box before the cross-country, as they had done at Punchestown, and tell me not to try and jump the corner as it had caused some nasty falls. No one let me off this time and the unappetising prospect clouded my enjoyment of the whole round. Every time I wanted to feel happy, as Be Fair's jumping sent a thrill and a sensation of achievement through me, I remembered that I still had to face the penultimate fence.

For once I remembered what to do when I did face it. I kicked and at the same time I held Be Fair firmly in balance. He popped across the corner with ease.

The Raleigh trophy was won by Janet Hodgson on Larkspur, and from our fourth position in the line we watched her receive her prize – a pair of Bernard Wetherall tailored breeches. I was delighted to be so well placed, but how I needed a pair of decent breeches. At that point I was quite glad that I had made another blunder of the timing on the steeplechase course. Runner-up would have been painfully close – and yet not close enough – to those breeches. If I had not been three seconds over the limit on Phase B, Be Fair would once again have stood above the bouncing little Baccarat and been second. The prize winners galloped their lap of honour and filed out of the arena. I jumped off Be Fair in the collecting ring and patted him gratefully. He had given me a year of undreamed-of success and now, I told him, it was time for his winter holidays. As I took his saddle off, I overheard Mike Tucker good-humouredly discussing Be Fair's performance with Mark Phillips. 'Someone has come to stay, dammit – that means one less place for the rest of us.'

Three weeks later Be Fair did not find himself lazing in the Appleshaw pastures. Instead he was carving his name in the records at Cirencester Park. He had felt so well and was in such good condition, that a fortnight after Burghley we decided to give him one more week of work and take him once again to the Midland Bank Open Championships; this October they had been moved from Wylye to Cirencester.

While I was changing into my pantomime kit in preparation for our dressage test and Be Fair was resting in the ice-cream van after another three and a half hours of working in, Mrs Sivewright, a dressage instructress and steward at the Championships, appeared suddenly and coolly asked if I was doing my dressage test at 3.00 pm. I answered yes, hesitating slightly because I feared that maybe she wanted to come and watch it. With her flashing smile she said 'It's now one minute to three.' My watch had stopped.

I grabbed the borrowed tail-coat, buttoned it up, pulling off a button in my haste, and flung the top-hat on my head – no time to fix up the false bun. I yanked Be Fair's sheet off his back and tugged him out of the box, scrambled aboard and cantered across the park towards the dressage arena, stirrups flying and reins flapping. Before I arrived I heard the bell ring for me to start my test. I had no time to gather my thoughts or my horse together and forgot to bang my top-hat securely onto my head. I went into the arena and had to remain motionless and very straight-backed throughout the test. I knew

Cirencester, 1972, Midland Bank Open Championships: 'We do it for fun' (*Clive Hiles*)

that if I moved the hat would fall off and Be Fair would lose a multitude of marks for he was sure to spook every time he passed it. As a result he performed the best test he had yet done and was ahead of all but Lorna Sutherland and Peer Gynt. With one down in the showjumping, compared to Peer Gynt's two, he started the cross-country just a hair's breadth in front of his nearest rivals.

My blood was up. As I waited to start amidst Be Fair's cavorts of anticipation, I recalled all the times during the past two years when Be Fair could have done better if only I had not made a stupid mistake. Now was my chance to do him the justice he so richly deserved. We pulled out all the stops on the cross-country. The whistles, warning of our approach, blew in ever-quickening succession as we sped from fence to fence. Be Fair loved giving every inch that he could. There were no horrid corners but big, solid fences, some of which offered awkward trappy but quicker alternatives, others which invited a bold horse to gallop on and jump big. A sunken road constituted the final fence to catch out any who had been lulled into the wrong frame of mind by the two Aintree fences shortly before.

Be Fair fulfilled the promise he had shown at Badminton and Burghley that year. He received his first fan letter asking for some hairs from his tail, shortly after he arrived home as the new National Open Champion of Great Britain. Mary Gordon-Watson wrote a memorable letter:

'It was lovely to see you two storming round the cross-country to rousing cheers all the way. It was definitely a popular win, judging by the vibrations everywhere you went. Your head must be *enormous* now, not to speak of Be Fair's. He *is* clever. Corny is *very* pleased but just a little jealous too – like me!'

With a whole £200 of my own, courtesy of Midland Bank, I bought Be Fair a present of a radio to listen to on our long journeys in the ice-cream van. The remainder I blew on a trip to the USA.

I was away in America when Be Fair sent a representative to the Annual General Meeting of the British Horse Society in London, to receive the trophy awarded to the horse who had won the most amount of points in horse trials that year. Great Ovation, twice winner of Badminton, had been awarded it the previous year.

Shortly before Christmas, bored with being away from horses for two months (the object of the trip), I returned home with one big battered suitcase and six packets of Life Boys – the American answer to Polos.

7 Ups . . .

'Be Fair started the 1973 event season as he had finished the last. He came out to win the Crookham Advanced One Day Event by a convincing margin,' the *Horse and Hound* reported in March.

Two weeks later Be Fair added the Advanced Class at Rushall to his tally – or at least for half an hour he did. After the fence judges' score sheets had been collected, the provisional results were altered. A large 'E' for eliminated was chalked up beside Be Fair's name on the score-board. We could not understand why.

When I had walked the course it had been flagged for the Intermediate class. I had noticed that five of the fences underwent flag changes to make them more difficult for the Advanced. It transpired that I had failed to notice the sixth and as a result we jumped the wrong side of the flag. Several fellow competitors did the same, and in the heat of the moment we lodged £5 for an objection.

Be Fair soars over the open water with his usual zest for life. Rushall, April 1973 *(Clive Hiles)*

Understandably we lost our money, for we were merely objecting to our own inadequate attention to detail.

A few days later, a list of entries with the order of running arrived from Badminton, along with the invaluable car-sticker, a yellow disc simply saying 'Competitor'. Without this, the police could prevent you from even reaching your horse, let alone riding him. There were ninety entries on the list and Be Fair was Number 61, indicating that his dressage would be on the second day, the Friday. How fortunate that I had already lined up the borrowed tails and top-hat.

Frank Weldon's report on Badminton was printed in that week's issue of *Horse and Hound*. I do not remember my inside doing as strong an about-turn reading the article, as it did when I digested the picture spread across the front cover. Last year's winners, Mark Phillips and Great Ovation, were jumping head on into the Lake towards the reader. The number he wore was 61.

Although I dared not admit it to myself, I had a peculiar feeling from that moment, a suspicion that Be Fair was going to win. In saner moments it was easily quashed – 'Don't be such a fool, Lucinda,' I would tell myself. 'There is no way you'll actually win Badminton. Those sort of things don't happen to *you*, only to other people.' I recalled the saying whose undeniable truth has always fascinated me, 'Man anticipates all, save that which befalls him.' I tried to think of every conceivable eventuality.

All the same, when my brother said his familiar baiting line about winning before I went to the competition, he said it with a difference. He said it with a barely detectable note of conviction. Instead of telling him to lose himself, I replied, 'Doubt it – you never know – we'll have a jolly good try.'

Motoring through Badminton village, the ice-cream van knew where to turn. This year Be Fair was stabled in the even more secluded Brassey yard, just across the lane from the Portcullis yard. There were only five stables in this one and no intruder found any of them.

Neither of us could wait to ride into the Park and hungrily absorb the atmosphere given off by every tree, tent and clod of virgin turf. I put on his bridle but not his saddle; instead I sat astride his best rug. Since Christmas, it had borne the name Be Fair, sewn in yellow across only one corner so as not to be too ostentatious. It was his Christmas present from his Gran and Grandpa (my mother and father).

Be Fair marched up the lane and into the Park as if thousands of people were lining it to watch him. Unfortunately so did Oliver Plum; my dignified 'walk about' was somewhat spoilt by being constantly on the alert for a particular olive-green Land Rover.

My mother and father arrived later that afternoon. As they drove through the village towards the great Park gates they saw a triumphant-looking chestnut horse, head held high, ears pricked as he stalked towards them through the Beaufort blue and gold ironwork of the crested gates. He was preceded by his little canine herald, white banner held high.

My mother absorbed the impressive picture. Then she turned to my father as he stopped the car and said quietly 'I think they're going to win.'

She was right.

Be Fair won Badminton twenty-two points ahead of his nearest rival, Eagle Rock, ridden that year by Richard Meade.

Maybe he behaved so well in the dressage because he could hear Colonel Babe's high-pitched comments floating out of the VIP tent, which stood near the judges' boxes. Or maybe it was due to having had his two furlong pipe-opener before, instead of after, the dressage, mingled with the habitual three and a half hours of working in. Whatever it was, the two days of dressage came to a close with Be Fair sharing fourth place overall with Peer Gynt, 5.5 points behind the leaders Mark Phillips and Great Ovation – once again.

Mr and Mrs Cook collected endless members of their family from around Appleshaw and came in a mini-bus to cross-country day, bringing Erna with them. Nanny had come from her home in Kent and this time was staying with us nearby at Wickwar. Jonathan the peacock had died since we stayed there for the previous Badminton, but no-one dared tell me in case I felt the previous year's fortunes had died with him.

Karol and her three small children appeared on the Saturday, each wearing identical red T-shirts with 'Be Fair' stamped across their chests in black. Even Simon, with the added incentive of a new T-shirt, wore one and came too.

'Frightfully common, don't you think? All those Be Fair T-shirts – rather like supporting a football side,' a mother was overheard saying to her competitor daughter!

Badminton, 1973: The Be Fair Supporters' Club: Karol, her three children, my mother, brother and father

The spring sun shone down on over 100,000 spectators as they teemed through the various entrances to spread themselves out across the Park. The stage was set, the crowd scenes organised, the supporting rôles filled, now it was Be Fair's responsibility to justify being chosen to play the leading part. The star was off his feed. He was not allowed hay because it irritated his sinus and made him cough. He lived on a meagre diet of carrots – the only thing that would tempt him through his nerves.

Starting him was becoming a serious problem to which we had yet to find an answer. As the starter yelled 'Go', at the beginning of the steeplechase, Be Fair reared up and ran backwards and reared up again. In those days there were no such luxuries as a small, comforting startbox surrounded by pacifying white plastic railings. I ride quite short for Phase B and I lost a stirrup and lurched dangerously towards his near side. Somehow, I did not fall off and he shot forwards as quickly as he had decided to run back. He caught up the lost seconds – he was a fast horse – and came through the finish well within the time. I was relieved, I did not want a repeat of last year where, in the final analysis, I threw away two places through a few time faults on the steeplechase.

Mike Bullen, Rome and Tokyo Olympic Teammember, was walking through the crowds as we neared the end of Phase C. 'Don't forget,' his voice sounded cheerful, but serious, 'ride every fence as if he'll refuse it.' More useful counsel than 'Good Luck'.

Dick Stillwell gave me some much needed confidence as he advised me of how the fences were riding while I sat on the grass in the box watching Be Fair as he kicked and fidgeted. In the box was the only time he ever lifted a hind-leg to kick. My mother was attempting to anchor him while Wanna was trying, and failing, to check his back studs and my father was not being allowed to sponge his mouth out with glucose-water no matter what persuasion he used. How impossible he could make himself

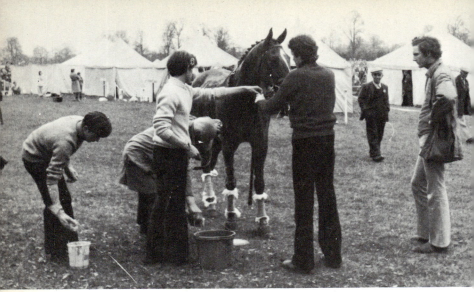

In the 'box' at Badminton. Be Fair is refreshed

when he so desired. Memories of Reform school shot swiftly across my mind.

The cross-country course ran in the reverse direction to the previous time and being post-Olympic year I had imagined that it would be more straightforward. Indeed after walking it three times I did not feel particularly intimidated. That had worried me though. I had learnt that I rode a little better if I was frightened. I do not know why this is; maybe it is associated with the adrenalin that fear produces, which must be needed to produce an extra quick reaction. The only comment I had written in the cross-country section of my programme was, 'NB Red flag always on the right of a fence as you approach it.'

By the time I arrived at the end of Phase C, I was very worried. Competitors had been coming home off the cross-country with cricket scores of penalties. Many had not completed it and poor Sue Faulkner's Sir Galahad had died after breaking his neck jumping the innocuous-looking hedges across Luckington Lane. The course

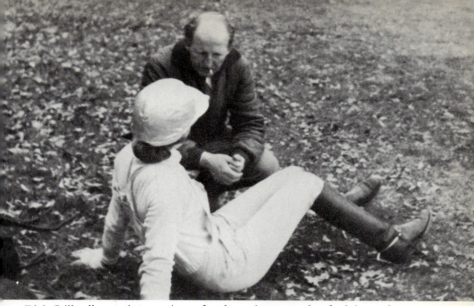

Dick Stillwell crouches to give a few last-minute words of advice and encouragement

was evidently not riding well. I recalled Mike Tucker's drinks party the previous evening; there I had gathered that everyone else thought the course was horrible. However I was comparatively inexperienced and through having a tremendous partnership with Be Fair and huge confidence in him I was somewhat blinded to the horrors the others were aware of.

My eyes were gradually opened as the course unfolded beneath us.

The third fence was the infamous coffin, which had been out of play for the first time in twenty-four years on our previous visit. Out of the sixty-nine starters, it caused trouble for thirty-one horses, nine of them being eliminated. It was through a vital piece of prompting from the wings by our Heavenly Producer that Be Fair did not add to the number. He was not wearing a running martingale. He had not worn one at Rushall and had felt all right, so I hoped that maybe he had grown out of needing one. He certainly had not. As he approached the coffin he threw his head high up into the air as I slowed him to the necessary bouncy short canter. He kept it there and never looked down at the three foot high stout rail, which formed the first element, until he breasted it. Then he slithered over at an acute angle to the left, thus avoiding facing the ditch at the bottom of the bank. In order to go between the flags and yet not cross my tracks, which would incur twenty penalties, I had to persuade Be Fair to turn hard right, creep into the ditch and walk along the bottom. He then had to swing left on his haunches, clamber out of the slush and mud and somehow conjure up enough instant impulsion to jump up the near-vertical bank out over even higher rails at the summit.

A loud cheer and much clapping from an amazed audience sent us on our way as we left a generous portion of expensive vaseline on both elements of the coffin. Fleetingly, I wondered how that would have appeared to a seven-year-old child, if it had been standing in the bottom of the ditch at one end, as I had been a dozen years before.

Drop after drop after drop. That was my principal memory of the 1973 Badminton cross-country course. In my programme I had marked a big 'D' by the side of the sketch of every such fence. Twelve 'D's appeared in the first twenty-six fences. Not just plain 6'-8' drops onto flat ground, but ones into the face of rising ground as well. A horse was punished for every bold jump he took, or was knocked over if he jumped cautiously and therefore landed at too acute an angle. It was only mid-April and the ground was not firm; nonetheless I could feel the jar shudder up Be Fair's legs and through his body, as time and again he was ill-rewarded for his fearless jumping.

I rode for our lives. Be Fair needed help. As the warning whistle blew I felt him need me, need me to hold him together before each fence. To give him the positive signals with my whip to which he was accustomed. He needed me to lean back in order to help him regain his balance when he stumbled and juddered on landing. And he needed to feel the vibrations of the vehement and enthusiastic crowd as he successfully negotiated each trap. A pat on the neck, a word such as 'brilliant' in his ear and he would take heart for the next challenge.

With three-quarters of the course behind us, or rather above us, there were no more drops, only big Badminton fences of enormous dimensions. A horse whose confidence had been drained by the rigours of the earlier obstacles would not have faced them. Be Fair still trusted me, his ears were still tightly pricked. He soared across each one and left the final fence, the Whitbread Bar, behind him to record the fastest clear round of the day. There were only thirty finishers, and only eight clear rounds out of the sixty-nine starters.

BE FAIR LOOKS SET FOR WHITBREAD TROPHY was the headline in the *Sunday Telegraph*.

The Duke of Beaufort approached as I led Be Fair round the main stable yard, waiting for our turn to be called up in front of the inspection panel on Sunday morning:

'I thought your horse looked the fittest and the best here when I saw him at the first inspection on Thursday. Now I know my eyes were not deceiving me. He went beautifully yesterday, didn't he?' He patted Be Fair almost fondly. Be Fair looked the other way as if meeting a Duke was an everyday occurrence. I continued to lead him round the yard and looked at the thirty survivors who remained in the fight. It surprised me that only one other horse caught my eye. I realised that it was the same horse I had watched schooling in the Park a few days earlier. I remember telling my mother that, to my mind, I had only ever seen two horses that I felt were the ideal type of Three Day Eventer. One was Be Fair, the other was a bay horse named George. Four years later, with Be

Fair in enforced retirement, George's owner, Mrs Straker, asked me to ride him at Badminton. He won.

There is a long time to fill in between the vets' inspection at 10.00 am and the showjumping which does not start until 2.30 pm.

After Be Fair had passed the inspection with flying colours we left him with his temporary nanny, Wanna, and went to the Badminton church service. We had gratitude to give and one final favour to ask. On our way to the church we passed Richard Meade who looked knowingly at us for a moment. Then he smiled and said, 'It didn't do me much good last time.' The previous year at Badminton he had held a narrow lead after the cross-country, but relinquished it to Mark Phillips with a fraction of a penalty for time in the showjumping.

Be Fair relished the afternoon's grand parade of all the competitors in the main arena. Accompanied by the band, we were supposed to walk in single file and numerical order round the arena, bowing to the Queen as we passed beneath the Royal Box. Meanwhile the commentator ran systematically through the names and placings of each horse and rider. As Be Fair showed off, swinging sideways and refusing to walk, I heard, 'Number 61 ... Be Fair, ridden by Lucinda Prior-Palmer, at present lying in first place ... Number 63 Belle Grey, ridden by ...' I did not hear any more. 'At present lying first ... at present lying first ... how right you are,' I thought. 'At *present* lying first – in the future lying ... fourth? ... or fifth? ... or even ... nowhere? What will happen in the showjumping – something frightful? Or will he go clear?'

Waiting – I watched the others jump their rounds. It increased the tension but I made myself study a few to learn from their mistakes. Be Fair had suppled up well with Dick Stillwell's help and now Wanna was leading him quietly around the outer collecting ring. Waiting.

Watching and waiting as earlier competitors jump their rounds

Most of the ten highest-placed competitors jumped clear and I began to feel that if they could, then I could too. In the interim there was only the waiting.

Marjorie Commerford and The Ghillie were lying in second place and they jumped their round as Be Fair had his final warm-up, helped by Dick, outside. She left the arena as we cantered in. Her face told the story before the loud-speaker announced her thirty penalties. She had knocked three fences down. Suddenly that hideous, sinking, negative sensation was reborn. I did have two fences in hand but it was evidently very possible to

Be Fair is the last to jump (*Clive Hiles*)

knock down three. Be Fair jumped and I hoped. As we turned to the penultimate fence a thought escaped, 'It's nearly over, we're nearly round, it's nearly all right.' 'No,' thundered the reply. 'It's a treble coming next – get the first one wrong and all three parts could be on the floor.' But the poles did not move. Be Fair's faultless round brought us the kind of feeling that words cannot sufficiently illuminate. The entire situation was a blue-print of all my most wild imaginings.

Bound in magical disbelief, a fairy tale was the nearest word I could find to describe my world. I must be Alice – this must be Wonderland. Once again I found myself thinking, 'This sort of thing only happens to others; it can't be happening to me.' And once again I remembered the thought I had had hunting with the Pytchley that day: 'Other people, on the other hand, are not riding

Standing out alone . . . 'This sort of thing only happens to others' (*Clive Hiles*)

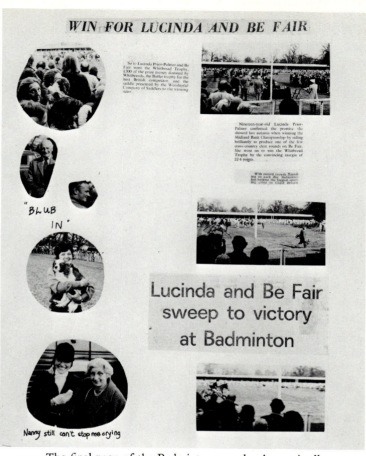

The final page of the Badminton scrapbook says it all

Be Fair.'

I did not switch on the radio to hear the news that evening as, alone, I drove my Champion home. Alice had drunk a great deal of champagne and she was still in the heart of Wonderland.

There are no radios in Wonderland.

8 . . . and Downs

The following day fifty-three telegrams greeted 'The Greatest' as we came to know him. Wide Awake sent him one, which although a year out, was strangely prophetic. 'Many Congratulations. Me next year. Love Wakey.' I remember it annoying me as in those days Wide Awake and I did not see eye to eye and I did not think that he would ever want to win Badminton for me. Through a series of informers came a rumour that someone somewhere was prepared to pay £20,000 for Be Fair. We never attempted to follow this up and find the someone. After all that Be Fair had done for us as a family, no money could buy him. I think this was probably evident to all, because that was the nearest we ever came to being offered any money for him.

Be Fair counts his telegrams – fifty-three in all (*Keystone Press*)

The newspapers went mad with joy when the short-list for the European Championships in Kiev was announced. Not only was Princess Anne on it, but there was not one single man amongst the ten of us. 'Meade without Mount – All ladies for Kiev.' They had the greatest fun printing more or less hideous photographs and tagging each of them with dreadful catch phrases. Sue Hatherly was labelled 'the beautiful blonde from Bletchley'. The diminutive and feminine Ginny Thompson was apparently, 'one of the toughest and most dedicated event riders in the country'. 'High-stepping young girl from Hampshire' was tacked onto a photograph of me skipping. Perhaps the most direct hit and certainly the funniest was a cartoon which appeared in the *Daily Mail*, at least three weeks before the Royal Engagement leaked out.

A comment on the Kiev short list from an observant *Daily Mail* cartoonist

Richard Meade became the Henry VIII when he and Wayfarer were added to the list several weeks later.

My sister gave me my own tailored tail-coat and my aunt gave me her own pre-war, silk top-hat. I had to buy another pair of breeches myself, nylon, stretchy and cheap. But I had won that saddle at Badminton. At last

I had my own proper jumping saddle – this time model '73. Model '69 had been a great improvement on my father's pre-war hunting saddle and I had ridden my first Badminton on it, but it was really no more than a post-war edition in the same style. Then for Badminton that year Mike Bullen had lent me his own cherished saddle, which had seen both Rome and Tokyo Olympics, as for some time I had been told that mine was not helping to improve my riding. I did not need any persuasion to agree. Now finally I had a new one of my own.

In order to return a little nearer to Earth and generally unwind, I spent some of my £300 first prize in flying to the South of France. During my two week holiday I wrote a poem to Be Fair.

> Humbly he starts at the base
> Beginning his climb up and up
> onto and over the sturdy branches of experience.
> Suddenly the world begins to notice a shaking of leaves
> some fall – others part
> to make way for him.
> Precariously balancing on a leaf at the top
> A leaf that will fall unhindered to the ground
> when blown by that wind of ill-Fate.

I did not like coming back to Earth. The tables had turned quickly on us. No longer were we the young, up-and-coming Junior Team protégés. We had struck the top. A top performance would now be expected of us, or the vultures would be quick to swoop in and pick up the juicy morsels of the chant 'It was only a fluke.' Already my own vulture had started a soft chorus of self-doubt. I did not feel that I had deserved such fortune; I did not feel particularly proficient at Three Day Eventing – just very lucky. One newspaper had described us as having had a 'meteoric rise to fame', and that was exactly the problem. It had all happened so quickly, too quickly – how could it possibly continue?

Summer, 1973: Be Fair with his trophies – Oliver Plum feels it has been a combined effort

By letter, I heard that a very portly Be Fair was languishing in fields of tall grass with his back shoes taken off. He at least was thoroughly unperturbed as he enjoyed his holiday.

'Your beautiful red son sends you a langorous wave of his fore-leg from his hammock and says he loves you very much. He says he doesn't think retirement will be so bad after all!!'

On returning home it proved to be a difficult summer to train a horse in. The weather was hot, the ground was parched and Be Fair jumped very little. He went a few times to Pat's small rented field for her to help him with suppling exercises over her tin cans and poles. Pat still bursts into laughter whenever she recalls the first time she was mentioned in print. Shortly after Badminton that year I had referred to the years of tremendous guidance that she had given Be Fair and me and described her as having 'an enormous family, a few tin cans and lots of common sense'.

Through the constant generosity of local racehorse trainer Toby Balding, we had unlimited use of nine furlongs of cushion-like shavings gallops. Fitness work, therefore, was able to continue without worrying about jarring his legs. Others were less fortunate and when in August we arrived at the Osberton Two Day Event in Nottinghamshire for the final team trial, our friends Corny and Mary and Ginny Thompson and Cornish Duke, were missing. Corny had contracted a cough and Cornish Duke had gone lame.

A refusal across country at the fence on the river bank, which eliminated HRH and Doublet and stopped many others, dropped us back to fifth place after being placed second in the dressage. It gave me a needed reminder not to switch on to automatic, but despite that, the ticket to Kiev was confirmed.

Before flying, the final six as well as HRH and Goodwill, who was invited to defend her 1971 European title, concentrated at Ascot for a week's training. In the selectors' minds the principal objective for this week was to ensure that they were sending abroad a team of horses fit and sound enough to win.

Peter Scott-Dunn had possibly forgotten how unlevel behind Be Fair had been all his life if he was trotted out first thing in the morning. He was suitably shocked and it took him some time to convince himself that this was only Be Fair, how he always had been and how he always would be. Mr Mactimmony had noted the same muscle wastage on one side of his pelvis as had the vets. We continued to have his back checked and the necessary vertebrae replaced by Mr Herrod Taylor, an ex-pupil of Mr Mactimmony, who lived within easy reach of home. Despite this, he never trotted up level unless he was warmed up and nearly always had a stride or two of unlevelness in a dressage test.

As well as having two long gallops around the unforgivingly hard Ascot Racecourse, David came over during the week to help with our dressage. We felt well prepared therefore for our first senior international adventure.

There is a distinct feeling of graduation on leaving the Junior Team for the Senior Team. Instead of a simple summer-sheet indicating his patronage, each horse had a complete kit covered with Union Jacks. Rugs, sheets, padded head collars especially designed for flying, bandages, tail-guards, string vests and coolers were all to be taken with him in a wickerwork laundry hamper. I discovered to my disappointment, that this beautiful pale blue trousseau was only lent, and spent the remainder of the year under B.H.S. lock and key.

Most of the morning before we left I spent in the hot sun outside Be Fair's stable, packing odds and ends along with his new uniform, into the hamper. Occasionally he would peer over the door and look enquiringly at the new colour scheme. If he noticed I was watching him he would quickly change his gaze to something over the other side of the yard or withdraw his head pretending to be disinterested. Shortly before midday, I was approached by Colonel Bill Lithgow, the evergreen chef d'équipe with a white moustache, to whom I had as a runner delivered Colonel Moseley's message during the European Championships at Burghley, two years previously. I stood up as the hamper was almost full and I was quietly gloating that I had been able to finish an hour before the loading was due to commence. I had already been ticked off once that week by the Colonel for being late for a meeting.

'Nearly done? – Jolly good, well done – Um, you must have done a neat job in there – it doesn't look as over-crowded as the others. Got both your saddles in all right have you?'

Of course I had not. I had not realised that the hamper was to be filled with every single article that the horse needed and preferably my black riding-boots as well. When flying, I was told, space is limited and nothing can be left loose or lying around in the hold.

As I tipped the hamper on its side and let everything fall onto the concrete, I giggled to myself. 'The labours of being a learner – but it's all *so* exciting.'

Dawn showed some cracks in the sky as the seven of us stumbled out of the mini-bus and onto the tarmac at Luton Airport's cargo loading bay. The horses had been driven to within twenty yards of the plane. I led Be Fair into the travel crate feeling certain that he would not load. I wanted to be with him if he misbehaved. To our astonishment he walked straight in and ducked his head under the canvas roof, which prevented him watching the ground drop away as the crate was fork-lifted twenty feet into the air and then slid on ball-bearings into the body of the plane. He did not have a friend beside him, so that he would not become jealous of them eating hay. He had not been allowed hay since two months before Badminton, owing to the irritation its dust caused his sinus and the coughing which would follow. I had discovered some lush green grass at Ascot and had cut him a net before we had left to occupy him for the first couple of hours of the five hour flight.

The plane had to land in Vienna for half an hour on some question of gaining permission from the USSR to fly into their air-zone. When finally we did land in Kiev, Be Fair had learnt how to brace himself and looked only a fraction worried as the engines roared into reverse and the plane slowed to a halt.

We prepared for a long wait to clear the renowned Russian customs. We had little hope of any VIP treatment, if the plane itself had nearly been turned away.

On the contrary, our passports were briefly checked while we were still inside the plane. As we descended the gangway we were faced with cameramen and formally welcomed with flowers by half a dozen girls, wearing colourful Ukranian national dress. Our horses were quickly and efficiently unloaded and taken off at speed down a three lane highway in, surprisingly enough, two smart, pale blue Lambourn horseboxes. 'Home from home,' I thought. It did not feel like Russia, at least not until we were deposited in our hotel, introduced to our rooms, and sat down for our first meal.

The bedrooms were as stark and lifeless as the food. High ceilings, blank walls, the bare essentials of furniture and two wire coat-hangers. On each floor of the large Hotel Moscow sat a hugely fat Russian Dame who guarded the room keys, would not allow any visiting after 10.00 pm and could not believe it when Princess Anne, in a series of descriptive gestures, asked if she could borrow an iron.

The first meal began with soup, which turned out to constitute the main course as well, for there were chunks of anaemic-looking meat to be found floating around in the bottom. The pudding was vanilla ice-cream and cherry jam, which did taste very good, although its delectability decreased as it was produced at nearly every meal thereafter. Along with sixty boiled eggs waiting in a row in their egg cups, as the breakfast-room officially opened at 7.30 am, was more cherry jam. It transpired that there had been a bumper cherry-harvest in 1972. Although we did not always eat in our own hotel, during the entire fifteen day stay there was only one meal where we did not have cherry jam planted in front of us. Janet Hodgson found it too much, and without a fuss she gave up eating and then became quite weak and ill. A small teaspoon of caviar placed on each side-plate had our expectations flying high the first evening. It proved to be vain optimism, because we only saw one other teaspoonful at the banquet which closed the Championships; caviar seems more of a rarity in its native land than anywhere else.

Be Fair approved of the large, cool Tzarist stables and it was convenient that the specially built showjumping and dressage arenas were situated close by. Training areas, however, did not meet the demand. Our chef d'équipe made it clear to our hosts that horses which were soon to be expected to cover over thirty kilometres in under an hour and a half could not be kept in shape on two bumpy grass patches the size of tennis courts. After two days, the Russians saw the light and made available a dirt trotting track a mile away. One of us forgot which direction we had to gallop in and it was fortunate that we did not understand Russian as the approaching trotter and buggy swung out dangerously to clear the way.

Being first to arrive, the British were alone in hitting all the blockades of red tape and lack of imagination. With much patience and perseverance they successfully bored a way through most of the barriers, thereby kindly leaving a clear path for the benefit of the teams from ten other nations as they arrived one by one from their long overland journeys.

The Press had its problems too. They were angry at the curbs on their freedom and at not being issued with instant transport to take them wherever they wished to go. They were given free passes to use Kiev public transport but it did not help them pursue the newly engaged Princess around the private roads of the exhibition park. The Russians had not much experience of the Western press and found it strange that they had come all the way to Russia to photograph their own Royal Family.

After each morning's riding, there was a great deal of spare time for the riders because grooming, cleaning or feeding was no longer their responsibility. In the senior team, each horse has to bring his own groom and I had asked an old friend William Micklem if he would enjoy the trip, and come and care for Be Fair. Not much older than I, he proved to be exactly the right person to have around because he saw the funny side to everything. As he maddened the Russians, so he delighted his fellow grooms.

The afternoons were spent either sight-seeing or swimming in the murky River Dnieper, where could be seen some of the fattest women in the world. Seeing the sights did not interest me as I had taken it in two years before. What a pity, I thought, that out of all the places in Europe I have not been to, the Championships should have to take me back to dull and familiar Kiev.

Following an afternoon swim, Joss Hanbury, who along with a friend had driven Lady Hugh's mini-moke out from England, and I, decided to return to the hotel via Kiev Metro. Maybe we overshot the station, as the Syrillic alphabet bears little resemblance to the Roman, or maybe we turned the wrong way when we emerged above ground. Whatever it was, each time we asked the way to the Hotel Moscow a Russian passer-by would point confidently in a certain direction. We walked and walked and eventually took a bus until we became aware of the town thinning out and began to feel that we were in the suburbs. Eventually it struck us that we had been directed towards Moscow, not the Hotel Moscow.

We did not arrive back at the hotel until late evening, to find that the others had nearly finished their ice-cream and cherry jam. They certainly did not believe us when we explained where we had been for the last three hours.

Without any night life or parties, ten days in a hotel is a long time and we were glad when the 'walk round day' arrived. After an incomprehensible competitors' briefing in Russian, we piled enthusiastically into four comfortable coaches of the kind that take a big party to the theatre. More than a kilometre of Phase A ran along the main Kiev-Odessa highway but after much wrangling by several chefs d'équipe this was changed. As we neared the steeplechase course, we noticed the fences were well built with soft brush. Although the silver birch frames were almost twice the usual height we were relieved not to find post and rails and stone walls, as is sometimes the case on the Continent. Relief was soon overtaken by worry as we walked the track and found it was like rough cement, criss-crossed with hard-baked ruts. Strong representations were again made to the authorities by the British, requiring that it should be disc-harrowed. Despite a repeated promise of co-operation, the afternoon before the cross-country day it had not been touched and Prince Philip brought pressure to bear. That evening saw a tractor resembling a railway engine, towing three trucks equipped with disc-harrows, chug up the main highway.

The coaches continued their journey, transporting us down the first two kilometres of Phase C. They came to a halt in front of a shallow ditch, between two brown furrowed fields of a collective tomato farm. The driver of the leading coach descended and studied the ditch for a few moments, chin in hand. To our horror he returned to his seat, put his carefully polished bus into first gear, revved the engine and took a run at the ditch. If he was not in hospital with a fractured neck later on that week I should think that he was packed off to a salt mine.

We disembarked from the immobilised buses and waited in the heat on Phase C for nearly an hour while sensible open-topped army trucks were called upon to rescue team members from all ten nations. Competition nerves were beginning to attack, and a sense of humour was running low. One of the ways I control my nerves is to make even more noise and laugh even louder than usual. I did find the whole situation that day very amusing, but I was told by our senior team member to stop being so happy. Apparently I was getting on other peoples' nerves who had less confidence in their horses than I, and who had not just won Badminton.

That word of advice, plus walking the cross-country course for the first time in the unrelenting rays of the afternoon sun, effectively changed my tune to one of a more serious note. We descended a rough, nearly perpendicular hill of wispy brown grass to find, twenty yards from its base, a large parallel with a giant ditch that stretched thirteen feet underneath. The conversation perceptibly dimmed as the teams digested this fence. No one was going to be the first to admit that they thought it looked fairly monstrous.

'Team spirit – must keep everybody's confidence high – do not forget,' we had been told. Judging by the way everyone continued their walk in silence, I suspected that I was not the only horrified customer. A little later on I quietly asked triple gold medallist Richard Meade a question.

'That second fence, is it quite big? Or is it that I'm not used to senior international courses?'

'Bloody big,' was all he replied.

It proved to be. Kiev unfortunately will always be remembered, not for its cherry jam, nor for the laughs and fun which we certainly did have, but for its notorious second fence. It was a course-builder's nightmare. There were twenty falls, and of the fifteen eliminations, two had a single fall and one fell twice. Had it been later on in the course and were it possible to gain sufficient speed by galloping across an open field, the fence would have been no worse than one at Badminton. What the designer did not account for was the fact that only the Russians were prepared to propel their horses at a headlong gallop down the four in one hill on the approach. Most of them did reach the other side safely.

Although it was only early September, the horses were clipped out so as not to waste an ounce of energy through unnecessary sweating in the hot, dry summer weather. Be Fair was chosen as Number 4 to go in the team. The selectors had reckoned, with Badminton in mind, that he must have the greatest chance of winning an individual medal. As only the top three scores in each team count, if the other three have gone well the final member can take the risks and go all out to win the individual title.

There is a small fly in the ointment, however, when one of the preceding three has been eliminated. Then the pressure is irreversibly placed on the fourth member, who must come safely home picking up the loose ends as best he can, and thereby holding the team intact.

I sat on a chair in the box before the cross-country, (there were no chairs in the juniors), and was briefed by Colonel Bill and by Richard, who had opened the batting for England earlier in the day with only one stop across country. I asked what the position was.

'Oh, not too bad. Go out there and have a jolly good *go*,' said Colonel Bill. 'There is only one fence you have got to get over,' he added, 'and that's the second fence. There isn't much room for the approach. Take your bat out and beat like you've never beaten before – you'll be okay.' I was aware that I still had not been told the position and so I asked what had happened to Janet.

After a short silence during which Colonel Bill and Richard looked at each other, my chef d'équipe said,

The notorious second fence at Kiev and . . .

'She had a fall at the second fence and then another later on, but she's round all right.'

I asked after Princess Anne. 'She fell at the second fence.'

'And Marj Comerford and Ghillie? And Ros Jones and Farewell?' They were both running as nominated individuals.

'Marj had a good round, just one stop. Farewell fell at the second fence but Ros was awfully pleased with the way he jumped the rest of the course.'

I enquired tentatively after Debbie West and Baccarat, our third team member.

'Um. Baccy said no to the second fence. I'm afraid they were eliminated.'

The message went home. As Be Fair was led to the start, I put my whip like a fishing rod in my right hand. It was something that I had never done before or since, but then I had never borne such responsibility before and I hope that I will never have to ride a fence like that again.

. . . our arrival on the other side

Be Fair cleared the second fence but fell at the sixth, a large six feet wide log pile hidden in the woods. It is still a mystery why it happened. He did not hit it with his front legs as he took off or the somersault he did would have laid him out across the top of the log pile. Be Fair always used his intense intelligence to look after himself but somehow, possibly through a trick of the light through the trees, he failed to realise that it was a spread and let down his undercarriage too early. I remembered nothing until I unstuck my battered knees from the trunk of a tree and looked round for Be Fair. There I saw him lying on his flank stretched out on the landing side with his head nearest the log pile pointing in the direction from which he had come. I thought it was the end. I thought he had broken his back or his neck. He looked dead. There was no one in the wood to help, only the female fence judge, and her child was with her. Both remained motionless, presumably with horror, throughout. Be Fair never liked to be approached when he lay down in his stable or field, I suppose because he felt undefended. I went to talk to him and to comfort him. He threw his head up on my approach and lurched to his feet. He was all right. He shook himself, pricked his ears and started to fidget, impatient to be on the move again. One of my knees hurt and felt unable to take any weight but the petrified Russian woman did not understand about leg-ups. Struggling with what little energy remained, I pulled myself into the saddle. The rest of the course was a severe test of courage for any horse, let alone one who had already been flattened. His trust did not fail him and nor did his heart.

 The British camp sent up a great cheer as we hammered through the finish. For a dreadful moment I thought that they must have presumed that I had gone clear. No one could understand the Russian commentary and the sixth fence was the only one that was not in the open and therefore could not be seen. Breathless and apologetic, I told

Finishing the cross-country at Kiev – a sinking feeling of having let your country down (*Findlay Davidson*)

Colonel Bill that I had not gone clear, that I had fallen.

'We know,' he said brightly. 'It doesn't matter, we're just all so glad to see you safely home.'

That was the only misjudgement of our partnership for which, while I do not blame Be Fair, neither do I hold myself totally responsible. The gold medal, which was apparently swinging close above our head the moment I had safely negotiated the second fence, swung instead to a Russian, as did the team silver. The Germans took the team gold and the British, 'mumbling through broken teeth and limping on bruised shins,' as a newspaper reported us, took the team bronze. We had become, we were told, the overnight heroines of Kiev. Although charmed, none of us could find much solace in our new title.

There were many consolation prizes. Janet was given a gold watch for the bravest competitor. I was given a small wooden box for the youngest. Be Fair was given nothing. A young and gallant Ukrainian presented me with some flowers so I gave Be Fair a pink carnation – he ate it.

Two days after devouring the morsel of caviar at the final banquet, the team and officials flew back to Luton with the horses. On his arrival home, Be Fair did not seem to be as radiant as he normally was. He had pulled a muscle in his back and his skin was flaking away beneath the short yellow hairs of his clipped coat. Dehydration, I was told, from the climate change and the flight was all that was affecting him. I felt in my bones, however, that there was something else that he was not happy about.

I wrote to Pat and told her my fears because I knew how much she cared about Be Fair. I told her that I felt the huge fences and the rock-hard rutted hillsides of Kiev cross-country and of course, the log pile in the wood, had taken their toll. Maybe this was the end of the competitive road for Be Fair and I told her that I felt he had probably

Be Fair was tired after his exertions in the previous day's arduous cross-country. I thank him

Be Fair eats his only prize – a pink carnation

had enough and that maybe it was time he took life a little easier. After an obedient and gay dressage test in Kiev, which left him and Larkspur leading the British to be lying equal sixth, I had promised him that if he completed the cross-country course the following day, I would take him hunting that winter as a reward.

By mid-November I had scratched any plans of going abroad and 'escaping from horses'. Instead I kept my promise as Be Fair and Wide Awake were tucked into the ice-cream van and, along with Oliver Plum in the passenger seat, we headed for high Leicestershire. Friends had generously offered us a flat and stables at Exton, and the secretary to the Cottesmore Hunt a much reduced half-season subscription.

During the first few days I hacked Be Fair over to where Mary Gordon-Watson was running a big hunter livery yard, in the magical setting of Joss Hanbury's William and Mary house, Burley on the Hill. She and Corny would join us for larks across country through the surroundings of one of the friendliest and most beautiful large houses I think I have ever known. Normally Be Fair would respond with eagerness to any grandeur about him. Neither this nor the inspiring presence of his celebrated friend close at hand helped him to rediscover his enthusiasm for jumping. He would refuse at a tiny post and rails; he seemed disinterested as he no longer revelled in his own power when he took off.

When I felt his wind was clear and his muscles hard enough I took him out hunting. There was nothing else I could do, either hunting would revitalise his desire to jump or it would not.

It did not happen immediately, it took three days hunting before I felt him no longer dwell at each obstacle just before he took off and knew I would have to put him in a double-bridle. He never became really strong at a competition, but out hunting, he was only the perfectly mannered lady's hunter, if he wore a double.

During our first day we cleared a fence onto a road and I have never before been bellowed at quite as loudly as I was that day by the Field Master. Apparently it had recently become law that the hunt were held responsible for any road accident which might result from a vehicle hitting an animal, which had escaped through a fence broken by a hunt member. I had no idea that I had sinned and therefore I did not imagine the roars were directed at me. I turned Be Fair onto the lane and cantered away from the shouting to join the rest of the field. The Field Master was doubly angry when he did catch up with me and ordered me to go home immediately. Chris Collins is a magnanimous person and he was at his most chivalrous that day. He piped up in my defence amidst a throng of a hundred steaming, stamping horses.

'Oh don't send her home Master, it's her first day . . . and she did win Badminton this year.' To which inopportune excuse a furious hail of ungentlemanly language was returned. We did stay out but kept quiet and mud-splattered at the back.

The following evening the Master, Simon Clarke and his wife kindly asked us to supper. I made another resounding blunder by letting slip that I had come up to hunt to renew Be Fair's incentive for jumping. A short time later I heard that that Prior-Palmer girl had told the Master that she was not interested in hunting, only in schooling her event horses.

I should think they were quite glad to see the back of us when we vacated our winter nest at Christmas time. However, Be Fair and I had had great fun. We had both loved our stay and what was more, my event horse *had* been schooled.

His fire was refuelled.

9 Trials and Errors

Hysterical was Be Fair's dotty girlfriend. Neither had an eye for any other when they were together.
Our stables were beginning to fill as 1973 bowed out. Hysterical, belonging to Mrs Ivory, would be playing the 'deb' next season as she started with her first Novice events. Wide Awake was already an Intermediate. And two muddy, long-haired youngsters stood in the field by the gate picking about for any last scraps of their winter hay ration. Help would evidently be needed if I was to have three competition horses and two youngsters around me. I did not want to break away from my tradition of doing everything myself. I felt that it was a step nearer professionalism and away from the truly family and fun atmosphere that had always surrounded Be Fair.
Be Fair's name appeared in heavy print in the 'Situations Vacant' column at the back of *Horse and Hound*, advertising for a conscientious responsible nanny with a sense of humour to come and help care for him and his friends. Joanna Capjon lived in the neighbourhood and at the time it was convenient to have her, but I did not want her. She was only just eighteen, under five feet tall and weighed less than seven stone. She had enjoyed as full a Pony Club life on her own ponies as I had, and therefore knew the excitement of competing. I felt she would never be able to put her heart into the job if she had to watch me competing and was not able to do so herself.
I underestimated her heart – the dedication that she poured into my horses and my whole way of life for the following three years was unequalled. Be Fair came to love and trust her as he did only one other. I was not

jealous; on the contrary I was grateful. Of all the types of people I might have employed, Joanna was the kind who loved horses in the profound manner which Be Fair found possible to accept. She became besotted by him.

Kiev seemed to have been swept under the doormat. Be Fair was tipped as favourite to win his second Badminton running. I groaned as these expectations appeared in print. Dick Stillwell had said to me in the summer, 'It's not so difficult getting to the top but it's mighty hard stopping up there.' This feeling had already taken deep root within me and Dick seemed to spur me on towards making every conceivable effort to stop there.

A week before Brigstock at the end of March 1974, scheduled as Be Fair's first event of the year, I broke my collar-bone at Larkhill in my fourth point-to-point. Colonel and Mrs Taylor had suggested I ride their horse Gribouille which has the unfortunate translation of 'Blockhead'. I had never raced before that spring and felt it was a challenge I ought to take on – just for fun. It did not prove to be such. I saw clearly the difference between the fear I knew before a cross-country round and that which I felt before my first race, as I walked in a circle behind unaccustomed tapes, amidst a bunch of tough-looking ladies riding wiry, lean horses on a filthy wet day at Tweseldown racecourse, familiar setting of the Crookham Horse Trials. I was genuinely frightened of having a pile-up while racing. The speed they go at the first fence, when all but the front line are unsighted is terrifying. And then there is the barging and the pushing and the shouting. If anyone tells me that I am brave, I am bound to disagree. A jump-jockey is brave. The fear that I constantly refer to in eventing, is not fear of falling and hurting myself, but of falling or refusing and thereby letting my horse down and making a fool of myself. Racing, you are not on your own and have mistakes from all the others to contend with. Eventing, you are alone and 99 per cent of the errors made are directly attributable to you, the rider.

Joanna knew something must have happened at Larkhill because I was late back that afternoon. When I did arrive I went to see Be Fair, my right arm in a sling and my neck bent in enforced sympathy the same way. My mother used to make me laugh by saying I looked like the village idiot, but laughing was almost as painful as sneezing. Be Fair sniffed at my sling and withdrew in disgust though he seemed to know something was wrong and was very gentle with me. I was forced to take his entry out of Brigstock. He sensed the lack of enthusiasm that filled the air because of this and behaved accordingly.

Bruce Davidson, Munich Olympic Team Silver Medallist, and his new wife were based at Wylye that spring, training their two horses for a personal dual attack on Badminton. I had met Bruce the previous year when the US team were training in England for the month prior to Munich and I had admired his horsemanship ever since. He agreed to have Wide Awake and school and compete on him for the next three weeks while I was out of action. Five days after I had sent him away, Wide Awake arrived home again. Bruce feared that he might break him down if he gave him any serious work. His off-fore was very filled and hot; the following day the other leg filled nearly as much. Mr Mahon, the vet, was summoned. He told us that Wide Awake was not about to break down but that his skin was allergic to the American cooling lotion Bruce had scrupulously applied, as part of his habitual care for his horses. Wide Awake had to rest his burning legs for three weeks and therefore, disappointingly, Bruce never rode him.

'Something good comes out of every evil.' Owing to the collar-bone and then to Wide Awake's allergy I spent some fascinating hours with Bruce being instructed in the various intricacies of a new fitness training programme. Athletes have used 'interval training' for some time but it was only at the beginning of the '60s that the French, through Jack le Goff, began to experiment, employing it with horses. In 1971 Jack le Goff came to the USA to train the Three Day Event Team; he brought his interpretation of interval training with him.

Its appeal to me was the theory behind it. When a horse is worked on tired limbs they are far more likely to break down than when the limbs are unwearied. I learnt that many leg strains begin, often inconspicuously, when a tiring horse is worked on limbs that are not sufficiently supplied with blood. In a tired horse the heart is more concerned with helping him breathe than with pumping adequate blood to his extremities. For a year I had been aware that Be Fair used to feel tired during the last five or ten minutes of a twenty-five to thirty minute canter. Part of it maybe was boredom, but nonetheless I did not feel completely happy about the routine I had adopted. I was prepared to listen to Bruce and thought that one day I might try out the theory, maybe on a horse that was not so important as Be Fair.

Three weeks after my fall, I was strapped up and rode Be Fair steadily round Rushall in the Open Intermediate. He was definitely becoming too familiar with this venue and I made a mental note not to take him there the following year.

The pre-Badminton issue of *Horse and Hound* dropped through the letter-box the following Friday carrying a lovely colour photograph of Be Fair jumping the Cross Question at last year's Badminton. The perkiness and enthusiasm he portrayed belied the punishment that had been delivered during the earlier part of the course. The article tipped Be Fair as being the possible 1974 winner. That night I dreamt Be Fair jumped clear around Badminton.

Although I tried not to be too superstitious, my morale was low. Firstly I always dream the opposite of what happens. Secondly I had noticed that from time to

On the front cover – a bad omen? (*D. S. Tuke*)

time in the past few years something awful was inclined to befall a horse shortly after his colour photograph had appeared on the front cover of the *Horse and Hound*. Johnny Kidd's grey horse appeared sliding perfectly down the Hickstead bank the week before he broke his neck when he turned over descending the same bank.

Fair and Square was pictured sailing over the big drop in Huntsman's Close; a week later he broke down irreparably as he landed over that same fence.

Shortly before we left for Badminton, my brother Simon sent me a very simple letter from New York, where he was working for a year.

Don't bog the dressage.
Don't bog the steeplechase.
Don't bog the cross-country.
Don't bog the show-jumping.
And you can't help winning.

Relief flooded in when I arrived at Badminton and found that the course was running in the opposite direction again and the Cross Question was not involved. Its next-door neighbour, the Elephant Trap, which shared the same huge ditch, was used instead. Only six riders out of the sixty starters hit their horse on take-off over that fence; thinking of the cover-picture I am afraid that I was one.

Shortly after we arrived, Be Fair and I had our habitual walk about in the Park, inhaling deeply the magical air. We walked down the hill and out through the Great Gates hoping that we might enjoy the same coincidence which brought such fortunes last year. But the approach lane through the village was empty, no mother or father were driving towards us.

Our number was 54, which did not give me the boost I wanted. Seven is my lucky number but it bore no relation to fifty-four. In the previous two years the four and three of forty-three and the six and one of sixty-one had each added up to seven.

Be Fair 'blew up' in his dressage test. He behaved appallingly. He would not make any use of the space at the judges' end of the arena. There was a whirring coming from between the judges' boxes – the television cameras had moved in a little too close. Be Fair was, after all, favourite to win.

I walked the cross-country course for the final time that evening, gritting my teeth as I approached each fence. I made a firm decision to take the quickest and therefore generally the most difficult route through every fence that I could. I felt that Be Fair had let me down in the dressage and he would have to make up for it across country.

Dick Stillwell gave me last-minute advice in the box before I set out across country and attempted to dissuade me from jumping the new 'S' fence the quickest way. I was confident that Be Fair could negotiate the trappiest but most direct route through the three elements of this innovative fence. I had watched in person the first eight horses of the competition at that fence and four of them had negotiated without any problem the quick route – a bounce followed by a stride on a downhill slope. To add to this incentive I had made the unforgivable error of not walking the slower route thoroughly enough to be sure that I knew how to ride it. Although by then, as I stood listening to Dick's advice, my mind was completely involved in the cross-country course ahead, the previous evening it had still been smarting from the feeling of humiliation following Be Fair's shocking dressage and I had failed therefore to even contemplate a slower route. Despair, I think, is one of the most dangerous feelings there is. It is one of the most difficult to suppress unless the capacity of its lethal sting is fully comprehended. Previously, I had not witnessed this particular kind of humiliation because before I had always been an outsider coming from behind. If the dressage went well it was a pleasant surprise, if it did not it was nothing unusual and went unnoticed. There was never any question of Be Fair having to 'pay' for a bad performance.

The BBC chose the film of the fall which we had over the 'S' fence as one of their 'horrors of the year' and beamed it across the screen before, during and after every televised event the whole of the following year. So there were plenty of opportunities to learn the capacity of the sting and to analyse why it had physically happened. Four horses in the first eight really had jumped the speedier route whilst I watched. What I did not realise was that only two others jumped it and they were amongst the next seven horses to come. After that no one else tackled it until Be Fair, who did nothing wrong either as the film clearly showed. His feet slid from under him as he landed on the steep bank which had lost its covering of turf and become very greasy. He was quite unable to lift off immediately for the second element and cart-wheeled over the solid rails landing with a tremendous thud five feet further down at the bottom of the bank. The only heart-warming part which the film recollects was that 'after they had both staggered to their feet the rider threw her arms around Be Fair's neck and gave him a reassuring hug before she got back on and they continued confidently and faultlessly around the remaining half of the course.'

Be Fair was happily sound the next day but he had the humiliation of jumping before lunch. There were a large number of finishers that year and there was only time for the top twenty to jump in the afternoon. Be Fair and I lay tenth from bottom. We had to stand in the back row whilst Columbus and Mark Phillips were presented with the Whitbread trophy. It was the third time Mark had won it and – a year too late for us – the first time the first prize money had been raised from £300 to £1,000. I mused over the fairy tale which had taken place in that same arena twelve months before. I recalled the last two lines of my poem:

> A leaf that will fall unhindered to the ground
> when blown by that wind of ill-Fate.

It is not so difficult getting there but it is mighty hard to stay.

Despite our retrogression, the chairman of the selectors was on the telephone the following week enquiring after Be Fair's health and asking him to join the short-list for the World Championships held at Burghley in September. Be Fair's health was, by then, perfectly all right. The day after Badminton however he had barely been able to walk from his stable. Mr Mahon assured us he had not fractured his spine or done any such dreadful thing that we imagined. Instead he had some very sore bruised ribs for a few days. He had fallen from a height with his legs scooped out of the way into the air by the unflexing fence. The considerable force of his crash landing had been cushioned entirely by his off-side rib cage.

Following the official preliminaries of the telephone conversation, the chairman, at that time Lord Hugh Russell, added that his committee had expressed a wish that if I was to represent my country in the World Championships it would be appreciated if I would refrain from doing a Harvey Smith at the fence judges. I thought he must be joking and I laughed weakly, though I could not see the joke. Unfortunately he was being quite serious. Before we had fallen at Badminton Be Fair had jumped up the three large steps out of the Quarry and hesitated momentarily on the summit before jumping off over the rails and drop. As he cantered away from the fence, in a moment of desperation as I saw the final hopes of saving the Badminton title sink forever, I swept my arm through the air and pointed back at the fence, meaning 'He didn't step back, did he?' I was sure that he had not stepped back and wanted to ensure the judges were in no doubt either. What I did not know was that twenty penalties are awarded for a definite hesitation as well as a step back.

I was grateful that they were still prepared to believe that our form at Kiev and Badminton was only a temporary setback. Both Be Fair and I must now do all we could to prove them right.

In June I drove to Germany to try to educate myself

instead of lazing about in the South of France once again. Hans Günter Winkler, the German showjumping ace who has won more gold medals than he owns fingers on one hand, agreed to help me for two weeks, ostensibly with my showjumping. We were all becoming a little bored with my lack of expertise in this phase. It was becoming increasingly evident that only Be Fair was prepared to make amends for my misdemeanours. Future horses might not – Wide Awake did not. The month before Wakey had knocked two fences down at Tidworth and dropped from first to fourth place.

Winkler found it evident too. The third day I was at Warendorf he asked me, 'Vot did they say you had done? Did they say you 'ad won Badminton? Vot sort of a horse iz he then, thiz Be Fair, if he can win Badminton in spite of you?'

I did not return home a well polished showjumper and still unfortunately have not grasped the technique as I would like to. During those two weeks, through riding different horses for the first time and being under the constant surveillance of a man who is as skilful a teacher as he is rider, I began to see a crack of light in the dark shroud clothing the mysteries of the 'art of riding'. I did not notice much more light until I returned three years later to Germany's top dressage centre. A slightly wider chink appeared after a month's stay there, but a shroud still hides the greater part of the secret.

I had always known my limitations and realised that any success Be Fair and I had was due to his unique ability and the firm partnership we had formed together. My aim has never been a gold medal, it has always felt too defined and fickle a goal. It may sound facetious but my principal aim is to learn, in the end, how to ride. It is a simple philosophy. If every horse that a person sits on performs beautifully for him then presumably he can consider himself an artist. Maybe then any success that he enjoys is not gained through that transient quantity

Luck, but through the imperishable quality of skill. Then and only then I imagine he feels true satisfaction and no longer faces the future sitting astride a piece of fluff, which can be blown from under him whenever that wind of ill fate should choose.

Hans Winkler was the only person actually prepared to tell me what I and no doubt others already knew.

'You are not a natural artist.' At the same time no one has ever told me before that 'riding is an art that *can* be taught – I had to learn.' If Hans Winkler can say this then surely that explains why unlike many artists who are nature's genii, he does not simply instruct, he teaches.

The ground was very hard again in July and August and I jumped Be Fair more than was wise through my eagerness to practise what I had learnt in Germany and correct our mistakes. The day after he had jumped at a show and been third in a small B and C class, his front legs became puffy. One was worse than the other but both proceeded to fill throughout the next day. Since then I have looked after several horses whose legs had a habit of doing this every day and it proved to be of little consequence. Be Fair's legs were not a pair. It had always been the near-fore which had been the warmest for it had suffered some slight strain before we bought him but had never caused any trouble since. That evening I studied them very carefully. I was deeply suspicious because this time it was the off-fore which was the worse. For five years I felt his legs nearly every morning and evening and the off-fore had always been his prized possession. To my horror I noticed the principal tendon on the off-fore was no longer in its usual straight marginally concave line. It was imperceptibly bowed. The near-fore looked as if it was beginning the same trend.

Gloom descended but I remained partially optimistic because my vet had always diagnosed any trouble to be of less consequence than I had anticipated. He arrived and examined Be Fair's front legs the next day and asked how long there was before the World Championships. He cogitated a little and then replied that in his mind there was not a shadow of doubt: if I took Be Fair to Burghley in four weeks' time I would break him down. The bowed tendons did not worry him too much, they were results of him being thoroughly jarred up. It was both the check ligaments under his knees that he felt were suffering from accumulative wear, tear and strain.

 Wednesday, August 14th, 1974. Doomsday.

Followed by the vet's diagnosis this was all that was written in the big diary in which I kept a daily account of the horses' activities.

 Sunday, August 18th. Dauntsy One Day Event.
 Be Fair and Hysterical.

I crossed out Be Fair's name and scrawled across the page, 'What a hope. No Dauntsy for Be Fair.' It was the only competition he missed through unsoundness in seven years of eventing.
 I went to Dauntsy all the same as Hysterical was entered in the Novice. Rumours spread quickly and that day many people sympathised with me over Be Fair going wrong. The only cheerful reply I could summon up was that it was a comparatively small price to pay for five wonderful years without any leg trouble at all. Watching the water jump I saw Colonel Babe perched on his shooting-stick on the riverbank. I think he was on his shooting-stick, it was often hard to determine whether he was perched or standing. I overheard him say to someone who was with him, 'Um, Bi Fair's finished you know? Won't ever event again.'
 Be Fair stood by the hose-pipe munching the soaked hay, which we had found he was able to digest without irritating his sinus. Every evening his fore-legs were hosed, every morning I took him for a short walk on the

road and then put him in the horse-box and took him five miles away to stand in the nearest river. The cold water drove away much of the filling and the heat. The tendons straightened out.

It was four days before the final team trial at Osberton and one week since the trouble had begun. His legs looked much cleaner although they still filled in the evenings; ought we to have another opinion? None of us could be absolutely certain that he would break down if he was galloped now.

My father said we should have not one but two more opinions. Peter Scott-Dunn, the team vet, came to Appleshaw to give his advice. After examing Be Fair he gave him a 50/50 chance of surviving Burghley. He suggested that we should not take the decision immediately but take the next few weeks in stages, watching his legs very closely after each canter and gallop. He felt that in this way we could prevent any real trouble by seeing the warning signals and stopping the work in time. He decided that we ought to try to run him at the team trial at Osberton in four days time.

A 50/50 chance of staying sound. I was not happy. It was better than no chance at all – or was it? With no chance I would have no choice. Obviously I would not run him. With a 50/50 chance I supposed that I might but what happened if we hit the wrong 50? He would break down, he would be finished and if it was very bad like his sire he might even have to be put down.

Then Nipper Constance arrived to give his opinion. He squatted on the ground and studied his legs from every angle as he squeezed them with his fingers. He picked each fore-leg up in turn and rested its shin on his bent thigh as he pressed the tendons from all sides. He said nothing for ten minutes.

Eventually he stood up, dusted his hands by knocking the palms together, and said, 'He's all right – you go ahead.'

Before he had come, Nipper had decided that he was not going to leave me hanging in the balance, he would give his opinion and it would be either yes or no. He was prepared to believe that there was nothing critically wrong with Be Fair's legs and that they had just been thoroughly jarred up.

Two days later I cantered slowly up and down Toby's tan gallops for a tentative eighteen minutes, thankful that I had been experimenting with interval training that summer and was able to break the canter up into three sections of six minutes, with two three-minute walks between each. Toby allowed me to use three furlongs of the most sacred of his virgin turf gallops and I risked that distance of fast work. Be Fair was delighted to be galloping and was very strong, having become bored with walking on the roads for the past ten days.

That afternoon Be Fair was driven the four and a half hours to Osberton in Nottinghamshire. I had no way of knowing whether or not I would be driving him home again the next day, before the competition had even started. In the evening his legs looked all right. They were cold hosed for half an hour and wrapped up in hot kaolin. We must keep the blood coming to the legs in order to heal any jar or strain. The next morning Joanna and I did not say anything to each other as we held our breath and unstuck the kaolin from his legs – both still looked healthy. I met Bridget Parker, who had been a member of the victorious Munich Three Day Event Team, when I was walking the cross-country course later that morning. She asked how Be Fair was. I crossed my fingers and said I would have to wait and see but I hoped he was all right.

'If he does break down will you fire him or have the split tendon operation?' I had managed to put such thoughts out of my mind after Nipper's optimistic visit. Bridget was riding Nipper's horse at Osberton and I feared that she might have been told something by him that I did not know. My worry intensified. My stomach pitched a little worse.

Both Nipper and Peter Scott-Dunn kept a close watch on Be Fair's legs and the evening before the cross-country they advised me to go ahead.

During Osberton, Be Fair had another attack of starting nerves on the steeplechase phase. I was first to go in the competition and the starter had not quite sorted himself out.

'I'll count you down,' he said, 'starting from ...' Silence as he closely consulted the stop-watch in the palm of his hand. I was not sure whether he was going to start counting down from thirty seconds, fifteen or ten.

Suddenly he screeched a hurried '1 ... 2 ... 3 ... Go!' Be Fair probably felt me tense at this unexpected order. He did not go forwards; he did not go backwards. This time he went sideways. He crabbed at speed into the tall hurdle which formed the wings of the start and somehow entangled one of his front legs in it. He panicked as he found himself dragging the hurdle fifty yards up the hill in the opposite direction to the first steeplechase fence. No one could do anything to help. I could only try to sit there quietly and hope. Either he would break his leg or break the hurdle.

Little pieces of stick flew across the brownish grass as Be Fair plunged forwards feeling the jaws around his leg slacken. The yellow protective bandage on that particular front-leg was concertina'd above his fetlock joint, but it did not matter. He completed Phase B within the time.

The General could bear it no longer and made a plot. Through careful planning with his own stop-watch he fooled Be Fair into going to the start of the cross-country and arriving at exactly the second the starter said go, thus giving him no opportunity to stand still and begin his nerve-wracking antics.

As he was short of work we did not go particularly

fast on the cross-country but Be Fair gave me one of our best rides ever that day at Osberton. As he galloped down the hill in the woods nearing the end of the course, bounding with joy over the double of suspended logs, putting in three instead of four strides between them, I remarked to myself that if this was the last time I rode him across country then it was a fine experience to end on.

Later that afternoon Nipper bent down in silence to study his legs. When he straightened up he merely said 'If you were thrown into the middle of the ocean you wouldn't drown.' It rained a great deal for the next fortnight and the bone-hard ground became pleasantly good to soft.

To my surprised delight, Be Fair and I were chosen for the World Championships. Obviously we did not expect to be a team member but neither did we expect to be one of the two nominated individuals. It made no difference for the competition if I was a nominated individual or one of the six extra combinations the host nation is allowed to submit. However it made a great difference to my psychological state. It meant that the selectors had not lost all their faith in us and that they had not yet shut the door on me and tagged me as 'unreliable'. To them I owe an enormous debt of gratitude. Without realising it at the time, during Kiev I had set foot on a tight-rope, which traversed a gulf of self-destroying negative thinking. I was to take time in crossing it.

The team of four and the two nominated individuals were ordered not to take any unnecessary risks in the ten days preceding the World Championships. No other horses were allowed to be ridden in competitions and Chris Collins, much to his annoyance, had to withdraw a horse which he had intended to ride in a race at Southwell during that time. We felt it was carrying the 'preserve our riders' theme a little far but there was nothing we could do about it. We resigned ourselves to being pleasantly pampered during the week's training at Ascot. We hoped that none of us would fall down the endless polished stairs or ruin our temperamental riding backs sleeping in a bumpy hollow in a boy's bed at one of the Eton College houses in which the riders were accommodated.

One by one the grooms went down with a bug during the last two days at Ascot and the first two days at Burghley. Colonel Bill gathered the riders together once we had arrived at Burghley and ordered us not to catch the bug.

'In the army we used to say, "This is not an officer's complaint." So, do you hear me?' he said, smiling with his mock brusque voice at its best, 'this bug is not an officer's complaint and none of you will catch it.' None of us did but two days later Chris Collins sent a telegram on behalf of the team to a prostrate Colonel Bill as he lay in great discomfort on his hotel bed.

IS THIS AN OFFICER'S COMPLAINT. WERE YOU TAKING UNNECESSARY RISKS. GET BETTER SOON YOUR N.C.O.S NEED YOU.

During a midnight race at a fancy dress party held especially to entertain the foreign teams, Colonel Bill had fallen off his donkey and cracked six ribs.

Be Fair and I began the speed and endurance phase of the World Championships knowing that at all costs we must complete the cross-country course without a fall. Our future hung in the balance for it must be our last opportunity to prove that Badminton '73 was no fluke performance and that the falls we had sustained in the past two major international competitions were not to become a regular occurrence. The steeplechase was two straightforward circuits round the outside of a golf course. Unbelievably, I lost my way. I galloped fast down the 'finish channel' of ropes when I should have galloped through the adjacent channel to continue on the second circuit. I realised what I had done and pulled up to a medium speed and veered left. Be Fair half jumped and then broke two separate sets of channel dividing string as he careered across the course to regain the second circuit. An awful thought dawned on me as I was about to kick him back into his stride. I had a feeling that by diving through the finish I might have failed to go between the appropriate red and white flag. I pulled him up sharply, turned and galloped 200 yards back up the slope, pulled him up at the finish, turned again, asked the astounded starter if everything was now all right and galloped through the correct channel and off down the slope.

Twenty-eight time faults later, I started the roads and tracks of Phase C. I did not bother to look at my watch, it was obvious that I was hopelessly overtime. I knew that I had erased any chance of catching up on the thirty-nine places after yet another shocking dressage performance. (Before his test Be Fair had appeared lazy and bored, but the moment he was asked to walk into the ring towards the arena, he behaved as if he was at the start of the cross-country and had to be enticed, rearing, into the ring by Joanna with her lead-rein.)

I did not see why Be Fair should have to do any more. He was tired after being pulled about on the steeplechase course and no doubt because he had missed two weeks of his final month's preparation. It was only a month ago that I was told he would break down if he went round Burghley. Although this now seemed unlikely, it must still be a possibility. The going did not suit him, the hot sun was drying it out by the hour so the stickier and more holding it was becoming.

My father was waiting by the first kilometre marker to check that Be Fair's shoes were all still in place. He did not know what had happened as he had been unable to see my fracas because of the rise in the ground but his watch told him enough.

'Is there any point in going on?' I asked him as I trotted towards him. He had no idea what had befallen me but unhesitatingly and with enthusiasm and conviction ringing through his voice, he answered 'Oh yes, I wouldn't stop now.' He was not made a Major-General for nothing; his ability to 'handle men' sent me on my way without another negative thought. Instead my mind became filled with the challenge of the cross-country ahead. It was fortunate that I did not meet my mother; she had watched Phase B with her mouth hanging open. She could not believe that anyone, let alone her own daughter, could possibly be so stupid.

The briefing in the box was almost the same as usual, the small difference being that the rider was not the only one sitting. Colonel Bill was also, as he briefed us from a wheelchair. He looked awful and in great pain as he manfully continued to play chef. After he had asked me if everything was going all right so far I replied,

'Not really. Tell the rest to keep their eyes open in that mess of string channels that faces them as they come round that sharp bend on the 'chase.' He looked at me briefly, a little puzzled. No one else had any trouble finding their route.

The cross-country was a World Championship course. Every fence had to be ridden and it was rare to find one that was not either on a slight incline or a decline which forced the horse to make a continuous extra effort in order to gather himself together for each fence. Between the third and fourth fences I realised that for the first time in my life I was riding a tired horse when there remained in front of us thirty more fences and another four miles. Be Fair had always felt sparkling for at least the first three-quarters of the course and generally for its entirety. I had no idea if he would continue as he was for the rest of the course if I kept my foot off the accelerator or whether his fatigue would eventually tell and I would have to pull him up and retire to prevent him falling.

Neither alternative was very appetising. He took one massive jump after another, by degrees he seemed to forget his weariness and grew stronger and keener underneath me and he finished the course with a time which although not fast was quite respectable. We were clear round a World Championship cross-country course – what a relief – but I would not be able to explain away the error on the steeplechase course.

The Americans were resoundingly triumphant. The team won the gold medal by a distance. Individually, Bruce Davidson and Mike Plumb were but a fraction apart behind the Badminton winners Mark Phillips and Columbus.

Columbus had, however, sustained a most unusual injury as he took off at the penultimate cross-country fence. The Achilles tendon, kept in place over the point of the hock by four horizontal ligaments, had slipped off as one of the ligaments snapped. The next day Mark stood on his feet in the collecting ring, bravely watching Bruce Davidson and Irish Cap become the new World Champion. Columbus, swathed in bandages up to his stifle, was resting uncomfortably in his stable.

Be Fair had pulled up to tenth place despite the time faults on the steeplechase. I apologised many times to him and was glad that at least it was not ten from the bottom this time. I told him that he was, in theory, at least the fourth best in the World and it was simply that he had obeyed my useless piloting that he had only finished tenth best on paper.

If the British team could not win, then I was delighted that the Americans had. Some of the English had been quietly sniggering behind their backs over the precise manner in which the Americans conducted their horses' schooling, fitnessing and competing, under the strict rule of their French trainer Jack Le Goff. 'Too stereotyped, they'll kill any natural instincts to get on with the job', was a description that I heard. I am by no means a perfectionist myself and was as much anti-discipline as when I had left school at the age of fifteen. Nonetheless, through Bruce's careful and fascinating explanation of the type of training that he did and why he did it, I became intrigued with their whole system. After my disastrous Badminton I had decided that I would start my approach afresh and try to employ the simple technique of interval training before the World Championships. I had little to lose after all. I had failed to repeat my success at Badminton when using my own methods concocted from a mixture of three other people's with oddments thrown in from watching Toby Balding train.

The pre-Burghley week of training we spent at Ascot before the World Championships brought many difficulties. I had insisted on sticking to my new system but I had no personal results by which to prove its worth. I could only say that I had learnt about it from Bruce and that the Americans employed it. That was not particularly impressive because the United States' team had not at that point hit their winning form.

I had to cling to my stubborn instincts like a small dog to a bone. Most of the other riders would ask for an explanation of this foreign idea called 'interval training', and I would begin uncertainly and unclearly to explain it. At the first opportunity a phrase or a double-meaning would be seized upon and a joke made. Everyone would laugh and I had to pretend to as well. I did not enjoy the side-effects but I hung on to the bone. Once again I had Colonel Bill and Peter Scott-Dunn to thank because although they tried to dissuade me, they soon began to realise that if they forced me to return to the conventional system it would upset me more than it was worth so shortly before the World Championships.

The final gallop before leaving for Burghley was conducted in the pouring rain on Ascot Racecourse. I begged to be allowed to carry out my programme which had reached nearly thirty minutes of cantering, broken up with two three-minute breaks for walking. I was made to go last so that none of the other riders would have to wait for me. We had been cantering barely five minutes when Be Fair checked short suddenly. One of his front bandages had started to unwind and he had stepped on the end. The elastoplast that was stuck around the loose end instead of the tapes which I do not like to use because of the uneven pressure they can cause around the leg, had come unstuck when the rain had erased its adhesive qualities. Colonel Bill and Peter said nothing as I returned to where they stood to find something to secure both the bandages with. I set off again without a word being passed between us. The rain continued to beat down. Each time I passed them I noticed their clothes turning a slightly darker shade and their faces a slightly whiter one as no doubt they fervently wished that they had never been so lenient in allowing me my whims and ways.

Sheila Willcox always took an interest in her Fair and Square's son. After Burghley, she kept away and I only heard tell of her displeasure. She wrote an article in *Riding* magazine on the World Championships in which she afforded Be Fair a brief paragraph.

'Be Fair, looking the absolute picture of health, zest and fitness, lost his chance of success when Lucinda Prior-Palmer incredibly mistook her route on the steeplechase course.'

10 Some Put Their Trust in Horses

Ellie May belonged to Captain Naylor-Leyland. She was a lovely chestnut lady with four high white stockings, a white face and white spots on her tummy. Along with Be Fair and Wide Awake she made up the trio that were bound for Badminton in 1975. All three were prepared during the cold and very wet winter months by following the newly acquired theory from Bruce Davidson.

At least two-thirds of the challenge of riding three horses at Badminton lay in trying to produce all three of them on the day, sound and sparkling in mind and body, ready to run for their lives. The competition itself remained less of a challenge and more of a nightmare. However much I skipped, or crashed about the squash court I could not imagine myself being fit enough to ride two let alone three horses round Badminton. I knew only too well how cooked I was when I had finished on one horse after the cross-country course of a big Three Day Event. Nonetheless the opportunity had arisen and I must take it. After all so many things can go amiss in the preparation of a horse for a Three Day Event that I strongly doubted whether all three would in fact appear on the day.

Wide Awake nearly did not start for one. He and I were having a cross-country school at Lady Hugh's up on the Wylye Downs. We were supposed to bounce in and out of a V fence near its apex. I gave Wide Awake the impossible task of bouncing in and out of a 2 yard space between the rails instead of the 5 yard one. I had mistaken my line of approach. Somehow and with an excess of ingenuity the clever little bay horse negotiated the obstacle without harming himself as he slid over the second part, hitting it with his fore-arms. He did not fall but I fell off. I was furious with myself and wondered how I could possibly make such a wretched stupid error. Why should any horse ever jump for me again if I did things like that? A few more shreds of self-confidence were snapped. After a hasty apology to Lady Hugh, I continued into the friendly oblivion of the Downs and jumped a few straightforward fences before returning to negotiate the bounce in the correct place and without further trouble.

That was too much for Sheila Willcox, who happened to be spending the afternoon watching the schooling sessions. She had restrained herself at Burghley but now I perceived that she badly wanted to say something.

When the session had finished and we had left the downs, I made sure that all was well with poor Wide Awake, put him in the horse-box and walked over to face the music. I explained to Sheila that I felt nearly as desperate about my own stupidity as she obviously did.

She surprised me by what she said. Indeed she gave me a rocket and showed her displeasure but I did not expect to hear a compliment.

'You are one of the few people who have star quality. And yet you are just throwing it away by not thinking. Be Fair is brilliant and he should never have lost a competition in these last two years. The trouble is, of course, you won Badminton too early. You found it all too easy before you fully understood the intricacies and difficulties of the game. I don't think you really understand what a very demanding sport Three Day Eventing is.'

Most of what Sheila had said was a mere repetition of what I had been saying to myself ever since we had won Badminton. And yet if Sheila was prepared to say that I had this star quality, then somewhere I must have it. Somehow I must find it, nurture it and try to understand what it was.

Be Fair repeated the first leg of his 1973 double by winning the Advanced One Day Event at Crookham in March. Wide Awake and Ellie May both went well and were placed. Morale rose. We took Be Fair to Downlands Advanced One Day Event, where he went well but it was fairly deep going and I did not hurry him. He confirmed our suspicions from the last year that his salad days were now over. He was bored by the One Day Events, only the 'big time' animated him now. His legs were marvellous; there were no more frights like those we had endured prior to Burghley.

All three horses arrived at Badminton looking really well, but the Park did not look so healthy. Many of the elms had been executed owing to the elm disease. The ground was so wet and soft that every foot fall left a brown oozing scar on the grass. Down by Luckington Lane the mud was deep enough to spill over the top of all but the highest gumboots. Be Fair, I knew, hated the deep but I was hopeful that the ground would dry out in some magical manner within the following three days.

An army of highly organised friends came with me to Badminton. Each one, including my mother and father, had a file of typed instructions indicating a minute by minute programme from the afternoon of arrival through the four days of the competition until our departure. The logistics of competing with three horses at Badminton were complex and I am not a naturally efficient person. It had taken me hours to fathom out on paper when each horse should be worked, when each horse should be galloped, and what the others should do between each one's dressage test. Then there was four and a half miles of cross-country to be walked three times; roads and tracks to be driven and many types of problem to be sorted out. Who would put the cross-country protective bandages on the last two horses? I could not; I would be otherwise occupied riding number one. I always bandage my own horses so that if the bandages become loose and fall off or were put on too tight and cause the horse leg trouble there is no one else to blame but myself. Joanna had probably seen me doing it more times than anyone else. Much to her horror she was allotted the task with a promise that I would not blame her if something did go wrong. She was still having bad dreams over it most nights of the week leading up to Badminton.

The rain was kind enough to cease on the day of the vets' inspection, and so did the dreaded murmurings of cancellation of the event owing to conditions. The inspection was the biggest reward we had for our winter's work and planning. All three beamed with health and fitness as they paraded around the main yard waiting for their turn to come up before the panel. Be Fair was my second ride. I felt that he would benefit more if I had prior knowledge of the course from riding Ellie May, whereas I might well not be around to ride him at all if I rode both Ellie May and Wide Awake first.

With the ground as it was, there were several withdrawals and my carefully typed programme was completely thrown when Be Fair was found to be doing his dressage test at the beginning of the morning of the second day, not on the end of the afternoon of the first day as anticipated.

Be Fair produced the best dressage test of his life as the spring sun shone down at 9.30 am. David had come to Badminton for the day to help me as I worked in both Be Fair and Wakey. He had never seen Be Fair perform with such softness and submission and yet still maintaining his liveliness and sparkle. He felt as if he really wanted to behave and do his best. What a welcome change from Badminton and Burghley the previous year.

Later that morning with a light heart, I walked the course for the last time. Be Fair had gained a mark which would prove hard to beat. As I walked the sky darkened, the wind dropped and I felt a spot of rain. It did not look as if it was a passing shower and sure enough the rain fell continuously throughout the day. I tried to suffocate doubts about whether I ought to run Be Fair in these conditions. I hoped that maybe he had become stronger since his last serious venture in the wet three years ago at Knowlton. If I remembered to use my legs and four-wheel drive as well, he might not find the ground all that difficult. It nagged at me but I did not want to pull out, not at this point and this spring he was exceptionally well and fit.

In a good but wet frame of mind I arrived back at the stables to change for the third time into the pantomime kit. In my absence, another kind of storm had blown up.

The Marquis Mangilli, who had been one of the three to judge Be Fair's dressage that morning, had obviously started to wonder why I was coming into the arena at the beginning of the day on my second horse when the normal procedure for those who were on their second ride was to perform at the end of the last day. It was only then, with the competition already under way, that he rubbed his eyes and realised that I was competing on three horses. He left his judges' box at the first interval, to inform the organiser that riding three horses was no longer permitted in a Three Day Event under the F.E.I. (Fédération Equestre Internationale) ruling. He said that he would refuse to judge my third horse unless it was declared Hors Concours.

Who would want to go around Badminton in these conditions just for a school? I am no pot-hunter but my attitude is greatly enhanced by the distant prospect of a place and some money. Mrs Phillips was not particularly struck with the idea of her horse competing hors de combat either. On the other hand having managed to attain this point in the proceedings with all three of them it seemed a shame not to battle on with the challenge of trying to complete the event with the three – this complicated situation began to look as if it would be awkward to unravel.

Fortunately we never had to. Wide Awake was the last horse of the day and performed a satisfactory test as we searched for any small patches which showed green amongst the swirl of mud spread across the arena. We found few and as we sloshed out of the arena the loudspeakers blew water out of their throats and declared the 1975 Badminton Horse Trials cancelled.

Be Fair was leading, Wide Awake was eleventh and Ellie May fifteenth.

There was an air of deep despondency among most of the competitors. Ellie May's owner bought us some champagne and we shared it in the hay barn by the stables, with my team of faithful and disappointed nannies and with the American Roger Haller, who had trained for two months at Wylye before coming to Badminton to prove his worth for the 1976 US Olympic squad. His horse Golden Griffin, had 'blown' in the dressage test, resulting in Roger being placed the lowest of all the competitors. He calculated that it had cost him 1,000 dollars a minute for the privilege of performing in the Badminton dressage arena.

There is an anticlimax after every Three Day Event. Doubly so if it is abandoned before it finishes. It was treble the anticlimax to have three horses returned to their home stables, hard and fit, their adrenalin running high with the expectation of cross-country day. Be Fair and Ellie May had already been clipped out for the following day's speed and endurance.

Be Fair was angry. I have only seen him as cross as that when Hysterical was turned out one morning before he was, in the field they shared on one of their honeymoon holidays. For three days he would not speak to anyone and I was no exception. If someone should look in over his door, he would stick his nose out towards them, ears flat back and begin a series of mini-flybucks as he reversed across his large stable shaking his head up and down in his anger. The only other time he ever laid his ears back, before or since, was if he was either very hungry, or very fit and somebody was trying to groom his tummy.

All three had the same laxative diet and long, slow, road work for ten days to help them unwind and soften up. Be Fair behaved as badly as he possibly could. If he was unable to find anything along the road to spook at then he would imagine something. Through his own initiative he had developed a new habit shortly after he had won Badminton two years ago. It was called 'the Capriole' and was his high school edition of the 'whip round' which he had perfected in his youth. He still whipped round at the speed of light and with absolutely no warning, but as he did so he leapt high into the air, keeping his head and neck arched as he kicked out behind with both hind legs. It was very unseating and as it happened unexpectedly I often found myself propelled up his neck. He never jinked sideways in order to unseat me though. From the beginning he never had any intention of hurting anyone; he knew how much leg-pulling he could do, and just how far he could go. When my mother or father used to ride him, however fit and cheeky he may have been feeling, he never misbehaved.

With Badminton cancelled, the selectors had practically nothing in the way of guidelines to help them choose their team for the European Championships to be held that September in Germany. Be Fair's name was put on the short-list again. I thanked God for my father; without him I would not have gone across country at the World Championships. The unveiled memories of that steeplechase blunder would then have been written as my epitaph, and our names effectively removed from the short-list forever.

Later in May, Hysterical took part in her first Three Day Event at Tidworth. It poured with rain again and the steeplechase and cross-country were transformed overnight from bone-rattlers to treacherous skid-pans. Hysterical was still young and not well balanced. I asked her to go faster than she was ready for round the steeplechase course. She pitched headlong on landing over one of the downhill fences and we both skidded on our sides for thirty yards. Although she was unharmed, she had winded herself and I felt it better to retire her.

Two weeks later I rode Ellie May at Punchestown. We had two falls on the cross-country and only narrowly escaped a third. She was withdrawn before the show-jumping day as she was not quite sound. It crossed my mind to remember to tell Be Fair when I returned home, that even if Badminton had not been cancelled he might never have seen the start of Phase A.

Three weeks later, along with five other British, two German and two Dutch competitors, Wide Awake and I flew on an all expenses paid trip to Ledyard Three Day Event in Boston, Massachusetts. My sister, Karol, well remembers being told by me shortly before I left, that if I could not keep upright at Ledyard I had definitely decided to renounce the sport that in the past had brought me such unprecedented delight. Hanging by only a finger and thumb from the tight-rope of self-confidence, I imagined that whatever star quality Sheila Willcox was referring to had vanished with my teens. I was twenty-one and I had fallen five times in the last five major international Three Day Events. I could see no plausible excuse for continuing to burden good horses with my presence. I trusted them, but I did not trust myself.

Colonel Babe died of a heart illness between Punchestown and Ledyard. From treating him with trembling respect, I had grown to look upon him with loving veneration. His wisdom and understanding of people had guided many, especially the young. We knew how much we owed 'Uncle Babe' and Be Fair signed a short piece which the *Horse and Hound* printed underneath his obituary on the day we flew to the USA. If he had to die, I was quite glad that he had gone before he was able to witness the decline and fall of one of his protégés.

Ledyard Farm was a ten day trip to party paradise. To avoid the heat and the flies we rode out at 5.30 each morning. We spent most of the remainder of the day sleeping by or in the pool and eating magnificent cold food banquets. Nearly every night there was a party, most of which terminated with us all in the pool once again, generally fully clothed.

It came as quite a shock to remember that we had in fact been flown out to Ledyard for a Three Day Event. Hat boxes were hurriedly unearthed from under piles of damp bikinis, bathing towels and shorts. Tail-coats were eventually found on hangers which were lending their shoulders to bedraggled party dresses. The familiar old dressage test was hastily re-read in order to refresh the mind. The competition started.

The afternoon before the cross-country I felt ill and physically sick. I was told I had sunstroke, was given some pills and sent to bed. Each time I sat up I felt sicker so I stayed in bed. All night and half the next morning I slept until I had to abandon bed and go and prepare for the speed and endurance phase ahead. I still did not feel well, although no longer sick, as I bandaged Wide Awake's legs for the cross-country. I wondered whether this would be the last time I would bandage a horse's legs: the last time I would put my crash hat and number cloth on, the last time I would set my watch and check the roads and tracks timing sellotaped round my naked arm. No one else knew that Ledyard was to be responsible for the decision I would make on the direction of my future. I suspected, however, that my parents sensed its importance.

Trotting through the welcome shade of some woods on Phase A, I began to feel better. I was nearly run away with on Phase B, the steeplechase, which indicated that I was obviously not riding at all well or strongly. On Phase C I pulled myself together, gathered the strength I knew that I had and tried my hardest to face the test ahead with a sensible and mature attitude. Why should Wide Awake not go clear? Why should anything go wrong? 'Why should it go right?' came the reply from that negative voice inside my head.

In the burning heat of the afternoon sun, Wide Awake stood in the box, a short distance from a large heap of refreshing crushed ice, waiting to start the cross-country. I felt as tight inside as I had done at my first ever experience at a Three Day Event.

Half an hour later my father made a transatlantic call to my mother at Appleshaw. I heard him say, 'It's all fine – just fine . . .' They had sensed the importance of my going clear.

Things do not all start to go right at once however. I still had not completely clicked with Wide Awake as was apparent in the showjumping. We were lucky only to have knocked two down, because we hit six and dropped from fourth to eighth position.

Only as I think about it now do I realise how strange it was that the sunstroke only hit me ten days after I had been lying about in its rays. How strange that I had suddenly completely recovered by the time I had weighed in at the end of the cross-country.

Was it German Measles I caught just before my first Three Day Event at Tidworth in 1970? Or was it 'sunstroke'?

11 'The Greatest'

With the return to Osberton for the third year running in 1975 came a renewal of positive thinking. I was quite sure Be Fair could win the Advanced Two Day Event at Osberton and I had a suspicion that he would. I had never known him at such a peak of well-being; with the occasional 'Capriole' he stalked about the countryside with an air of invincible wisdom and pride, as if he was preparing for his finest hour.

He found no trouble in swamping the opposition and won this final trial for the team. So confident were we together that we relinquished our shyness of corner fences and took on one that was nearly a right angle. He soared over it, accurate to a hair, brushing the left toe of my boot against the upright of the white flag.

Janet Hodgson and Larkspur, Sue Hatherley and Harley, Princess Anne and Goodwill and Be Fair were the four nominated to attend the European Championships in Luhmühlen in West Germany, during the first week-end of September.

Be Fair and I were content: we felt the current had changed and was flowing our way.

The fitness work during the week's training at Ascot was a little less of a battle than the previous year. Although I still had no personal results to show and could only point to the Americans as a reason for using interval training, they at least were now regarded with a modicum of respect, since they had proved themselves by becoming the new undisputed World Champions. Colonel Bill had become acclimatised to the idea that I had this weird programme in my head and thought he had better let me pursue it. He slotted me into the gallop's schedule in the last place so that my 'tribal rites', as he referred to them, would not delay the others.

The principal difference between the others and myself was that they performed all their slow canter work either the day before or the day after through Windsor Great Park and used the two mornings we were allowed onto Ascot Racecourse, solely for a good gallop. The theory I followed was that the capacity for endurance is enlarged without ever putting undue strain on the body by asking, each time, just a little bit more effort than the heart and lungs want to make at just the moment when they are best conditioned to make that effort. Scientific research has shown that after a horse has been fully worked it takes three to four days for him to recover completely without starting to relax and let down again. This means working the horse on day 1, doing nothing but either walking or resting on day 2, increasing general schooling and jumping on days 3 and 4, then full work again on day 5.

A programme will commence roughly seven to eight weeks prior to the Three Day Event, following two to four weeks road work. It may start with 3 two minute canters interspersed by 2 three minute breaks of walking. 2 (3) 2 (3) 2. Gradually it will increase to 10 (3) 10 (3) 10 before the competition. The total amount worked depends largely on the terrain. The American team prepared for the mountainous Montreal course by cantering their horses on strongly undulating country covered in soft virgin turf in Pennsylvania. The maximum amount of minutes they reached before the games was 7,8,7. The speed is calculated at 400 metres a minute, which is equivalent to one mile in four minutes and is a steady working canter.

The aim of such a system is, essentially, to increase the expansion capacity of heart and lungs without putting undue stress or strain on either them or the limbs. Fast work over a distance of half to three-quarters of a mile is only introduced at the end of the last three to four workouts.

A few days before the team leaves its training at Ascot there is always a press morning with the riders and the horses on Smith's Lawn in the Great Park. I was finishing practising a little showjumping with Hysterical on the morning that fifty-odd cameramen arrived for their date. There was a rare opportunity for Hysterical to practise jumping a water-jump. The press men were in a heap about 200 yards away at the far end of the arena and all looking in the opposite direction, waiting, no doubt, for Princess Anne to come up from the stables. Joanna had not yet arrived with Be Fair either. That day was the last chance I would have to practise the water on Hysterical and I felt bound to do so.

When Joanna did arrive with Be Fair we swopped horses and she looked at Hysterical and me with an enquiring expression on her face. Hysterical looked as if she had sweated a great deal – but only on one side; the other looked fine. I looked all right on one side too. The other thigh, boot and elbow were filthy dirty and the off-side stainless steel stirrup was drastically bent. I explained to Joanna that we had had a little local difficulty at the water-jump. We had in fact taken with us the small, mobile brush fence that stood on its edge, as Hysterical had slid into the water on her backside because she had tried to put the brakes on at the last moment. For a moment she had sat in the middle of the ten feet stretch of water and then overbalanced and we both plopped onto our sides in the filthy but shallow water. I was terrified lest Colonel Bill or the press would see me. I knew the one would be furious and the other delighted.

I thought I was in luck; the press morning went off without embarrassment as I hid my dirty side and when, after an hour and a half, they had clicked and questioned enough and driven away, I gave Be Fair to Joanna and leapt back onto Hysterical. I intended to take her back to attempt to overcome our hiccough at the water-jump.

Colonel Bill spied me as I wandered off in the direction of the showjumps.

'You're not going to jump that water-jump again are you?' 'Oh dear,' I thought, 'he must have seen the first effort.'

'Yes indeed I saw, and so did half the country's press photographers. I tell you they were as quick as a flash to wheel round and start taking uncompromising pictures of you two thrashing about in the water. They only stopped because I stood in front of them and told them unflinchingly that in fact that was not the horse you were taking to the European Championships; it was just a very green one being taught to swim.' They never bothered to print one single photograph.

The chef d'équipe had no intention of letting me jump the water again. He felt it an exceedingly unnecessary risk for one of his team members to take. I, on the other hand, felt that I could not possibly leave Hysterical dwelling on such a bad note whilst I was away for a whole fortnight. We looked at each other and both clearly understood the other's viewpoint without losing sight of our own. Colonel Bill has not been such a successful chef d'équipe for a decade for nothing. He knew how to deal with his strong-willed riders. He knew when to be tough and put his foot down, but he also knew when to do so would cause a genuine upset. Hysterical was persuaded to jump over the top of the water ten minutes later and the following day we won our first 'Newcomers' at a local Berkshire show.

That evening, sitting in the drawing room of the private side of Martin Whiteley's boy's house at Eton, where we were staying for the week, I found that Colonel Bill and I were on our own. I took the opportunity to thank him for his understanding and tolerance over the Hysterical incident and over my 'tribal rites' on Ascot race-course.

'That's all right,' he grinned through his white moustache, 'maybe you'll be European Champion this time next week. Then we'll *have* to believe you know what you're doing.'

During the morning of 31 August, a convoy of horse boxes and cars left the Harwich-Bremerhaven ferry and sped through the town of Bremerhaven onto the Autobahn, escorted front and rear by flashing police escorts. Red traffic lights, stop signs, roundabouts: it made no difference – they were all treated in the same manner. All other traffic screeched to an unexpected emergency halt as a policeman jumped out of his car and waved a red lollipop at the oncoming traffic. Mike Tucker, riding Ben Wyvis as a nominated individual, remarked that it was a way of arriving in Germany, akin to the drive-round of the roads and tracks at Badminton, and it certainly set the pace for what was to come. Once on the Autobahn the police left us to our own devices. My ice-cream van chugged along at the back of the convoy, trying, somewhat in vain, to keep up with the two five-geared horse-boxes in front. It could barely reach 50 mph for some reason, probably because it was in a bad mood at being used as a luggage van and not a horse-box.

The Germans are a methodical and practical race and we were expecting things to be done properly. We were not disappointed. The horses and humans had all the comforts and facilities they could wish for. I had thought that most of the Kiev trip had been fun, but this excursion to Germany made Kiev seem like life in a convent.

The first party we went to was held two nights after we had arrived. One long table stood stacked with food in a small, clean and attractive Dutch barn. Teams and officials from the German, Irish and English contingent filled the benches either side of the table. I am not fond of alcohol but by the end of the feast it was becoming a joke at my end of the table to see who could persuade another tiny glass of evil Schnapps down me. I was on number twelve when the tall oval-topped doors at one end of the barn burst open and in stamped the Um Pah Pah Band of five jolly, fat men. They wore brown corduroy shorts, cotton shirts and braces, thick fawn socks held up with bright green garters and the whole outfit was topped with a patriotic felt hat with a feather sticking out of it.

The Um Pah Pah band played to us for half an hour; the brand new foundations of the barn vibrated as the fire of the Schnapps was expended on foot stamping, hand clapping and dancing accompanied by whoops and wails. The three nations went beserk with joy as we all danced together. Eventually the band left and the party drew to a close. Exhausted and hoarse with laughing and shouting, I wandered happily into my ground floor bedroom at the charming, oak-beamed chalet-style hotel that was accommodating the British team. I had not had time to shut either door or curtains before I saw Colonel Bill come scrambling at speed through my open window into my bedroom with a look of fury on his reddening face. From his bedroom window opposite mine across the alley he had seen what he thought was Karl Shultz in my room. What he had seen was Karl, rather merry, lurching around in the passage-way outside my open door. The German rider was shown out of the hotel and pointed firmly up the road to his own.

Bedside lights were extinguished quickly that night. Everyone was in need of sleep with the possible exception of Karl Shultz. I presume he never found his hotel; I do not know as neither of us spoke the other's language. I heard a tapping on my open window behind the curtain and went to see what it was. A bleary-eyed Shultz stood mumbling softly outside. 'Nein,' I answered repeatedly. That was one of the few German words in my vocabulary and I reckoned that whatever he was saying at that time of night ought to have an answer in the negative. An explosion from behind Karl made him leap round in the direction of the chef's bedroom. Colonel Bill came flying head first through his own window, this time wearing only a pair of pyjamas. He said something fairly firm to me first and shut the window in my face and then turned and hurried barefoot across the forecourt. The moon was bright that night, and through the window I could see the darkened figure of Shultz as it zigzagged its way up the quiet street. It was followed by shouts of the most dreadful abuse. I felt it rather lucky that Karl probably could not understand what Colonel Bill was bellowing, but the next morning the commotion had to be explained away to my team mates who had been so rudely awakened.

Be Fair seemed to be enjoying his stay in Germany as much as I was. We went for long gentle rides and surveyed the German countryside together. He ate ravenously, unusual for him once the event was imminent. His ears went back when Jo brought his meals and he stood eating with one front leg bent up under his tummy in his impatient desire to eat quicker. I only did one half hour session of schooling in the week before the event. I had found that when he became very fit he ran noticeably short of patience when being disciplined and I was much too unsure of the consequences to risk having a bolshy horse on my hands. Peter Scott-Dunn and Colonel Bill did not mind that I did not school him much, but they did object when I refrained from galloping either. I knew him and I knew how easy it was to send him over the top. Since adopting interval training, I had discovered how the horses thrived on a suggested pre-competition diminuendo. Three days before the cross-country we did one short sharp gallop of two furlongs up a hill to keep the peace. Apart from a similar burst after the dressage that was all the work Be Fair did while in Germany.

Before the dressage he still needed a great deal of

work to cool a little of his chestnut blood running at a high pitch through his body. Although he was at last learning to contain himself when he went into the arena, I still never felt that I could sit down and ride him when he was inside the boards. Karl Shultz and Madrigal led after the dressage phase. He and another German had marks in the thirties; Be Fair was lying third with a score in the forties. There were a few in the fifties but most had higher penalties. Unbelievably the British team led the Germans by ten points after the dressage and we were all as delighted as we were amazed. That evening for the last time I carefully studied the routes I was to take over the exquisitely built fences without noticing who I passed as I walked the flat four and a half mile course, trying to maintain my concentration. The prospect of the steeplechase course made everyone anxious for me because they were very worried that I would lose my way. They were not being sarcastic either; it was a twisty figure of eight course around which we had to describe a series of asymmetrical changes of direction. The fences were beautiful: big and soft and Be Fair pounded round each turn and flew over each fence with ease and grace. I neither lost the way nor misjudged my time.

Most of the way down phase C I sang inbetween saying a passing 'Guten Tag' to village children playing in the fields and gardens. One family gathered by their front door cheered when they recognised the British flag on my saddle cloth. I felt that the Germans cheering the British did not quite add up, but maybe they had mistaken me for Princess Anne.

My father in his accustomed light brown stock-coat, which he always wore when he was playing groom in the box, was ready to receive Be Fair who came in two minutes early off Phase C. Those extra two minutes are invaluable. Twelve minutes seems more than 120 seconds longer than ten minutes. My father assured me that he had counted the paces at the correct speed to the small starting enclosure and timed how long it would take him to lead Be Fair there from a given point. For a year we had employed this method and it worked well. Provided Be Fair did not have to stand still at the start for longer than one or two seconds he could keep his nerves under control and would not suddenly change into a speedy reverse.

On arrival in the box, I dismounted and was sat in the chair, offered some cool grapefruit juice by the ever attentive Mrs Lithgow, and duly briefed, very briefly. Janet had endured two more crashing falls and been eliminated. Princess Anne was clear and without time penalties. Sue had one stop and only a few time penalties. Ammerman, second after the dressage, had had one refusal and Shultz was on the cross-country at that moment.

Richard Meade had flown over to support the side and gave me a piece of advice which was to prove invaluable. He counselled me to line up on a different tree from that which I had intended if I were to succeed in negotiating all three parts of the Normandy Bank series on a left-hand turn without running out.

I went to the mobile loo to digest the information and on finding them unusually comfortable fell deep in thought. Richard was despatched to bang on the door and tell me that it was time I stopped acting like Rodin's 'The Thinker', and came out and went to work. Despite the tension I felt, this incident reminded me of the day I had locked myself in the loo at the age of four and refused to come out until the doctor and his beastly long syringe full of dyptheria vaccine had finally given up hope and driven away.

Emerging into the bright sunlight from the shade of the powder room on wheels, I noticed my mother standing waiting, her chores in the box completed. There is only one thing that makes me more apprehensive than riding across country and that is watching it. I knew that

Luhmühlen, 1975; European Championships: 'A sensation of sheer enjoyment as he leapt from fence to fence' (*Hugo M. Czerny*)

behind the sunglasses and calm exterior she felt even more tense than I. She used to say, 'I mind so much about *both* of you. When you are riding a different horse my anxieties are halved.'

My riding orders were delivered, they were simple.

'Go for it – the gold, girl.' And Be Fair went for it like a bullet from a gun. He gave me a truly wonderful ride. A sensation of sheer enjoyment as he leapt from fence to fence, sploshed in and out of the awkward multiple complex of lake fences as if he was a surf board and jumped the final difficult series on a sharp left turn with such accuracy and agility that it was hard to believe that he had not walked the course three times himself.

Shultz was standing by the finish. He need not have asked, for my face and jubilant patting must have told him the answer.

'Okay?' he asked. 'Okay,' I replied. 'And you?' 'Von shtop into zee vater.' Be Fair had shot into the lead for the European Championships with fifteen points or one showjump in hand. The British team had left the other nine nations behind as they stood nearly thirty-five points clear of the Soviet Union.

Perched on a land other than Earth, I sat drying my hair in my cosy bedroom in preparation for the evening's entertainment, a big dance and supper for all ten nationalities taking part. There was a knock on the window and once again I went cautiously to investigate. This time it was a white moustache which filled one of the small panes of the lead-rimmed glass. Colonel Bill had come to tell me that *none* of his girls were to go to the party that night.

'Oh but Colonel Bill we must – it's Phase E, it's the fifth phase of the speed and endurance test. If you don't go to the party you haven't completed the cross-country day.'

No amount of persuasion succeeded. He felt that it was his responsibility to ensure that there were three British girls fit and ready to win two gold medals and one silver the following day and not wandering around with a headache and cross-eyed vision. That was that. Mike Tucker went to wave the flag at the party in the company of three eminent spectators: Richard Meade, Mark Phillips and Chris Collins. All three had come out for the week-end to support the 'Britischen Amazonen'.

Somewhat seething we ate dinner in our hotel. Underneath our displeasure we could see our chef's point. Apart from two Irish ladies of less tender years than ourselves, we were the only females out of the fifty-five men in the competition and we were holding the key position. All in all we supposed that we were quite worth 'nobbling' that night.

In continued sweltering sunshine the three team horses and the two individuals came up before the panel of vets the final morning. Janet Hodgson was in bed with bad concussion and Larkspur stayed in his stable. Various foreigners remarked on Be Fair's condition as they eyed him being led around the court-yard by Joanna. None of us could remember a Three Day Event where he had looked more magnificent. His legs, thankfully, had never given us another moment's worry since prior to Burghley the previous year. He sprang up the asphalt lane towards the vets between a line of shady apple trees. It was plain for all to see that he was not springing through the air to show how sound he was; he was springing through the air to show that he was 'The Greatest'.

Alas, disaster struck the team in the showjumping.

Princess Anne confirmed her individual silver medal with a clear round but poor Sue Hatherley had an expensive thirty penalty fall when the sore-legged Harley missed his jerk at a double of uprights. She finished the course with forty-two penalties and the team gold turned not to ashes but to silver as the Russians reaped the reward for a well polished performance throughout the competition. As I stood on my feet at the entrance to the arena I was not sure if my eyes were telling me the truth as they watched Sue and Harley's mishap. I glanced over to where Richard and Mark stood watching. They returned the look with blank empty faces. I felt for Sue. How can you console someone when they know that they have lost their country a gold medal in the eleventh hour? Princess Anne was marvellous. 'Absolute rubbish,' she told Sue as the latter apologised. 'These things happen with horses.'

The exhilaration of a brilliant ride across country had been given way to a frosty apprehension by the morning of the showjumping. A small error and so much can be lost in this cold-blooded phase. I felt no less frozen when Be Fair cantered into the arena at Luhmühlen, than during the same moment at Badminton two years earlier. Be Fair stood still for long enough to allow me to bow hastily to the judges and then fidgeted and wriggled and asked to be allowed to move into action. In under two minutes time either he would or would not be the European Champion. I shut the thought out of my mind and ordered myself to get on with the job in hand.

Be Fair knew. He was more intent on becoming the Champion of Europe than any other horse on the Conti-

Be Fair, intent on becoming the Champion of Europe (*Hugo M. Czerny*)

nent. The papers reported a deafening roar as we came through the finish. I did not hear the crowd; I was already in Wonderland. Be Fair swept me out of the arena and down through a channel of cheering spectators. I had noticed my father on the way out: he was pulling a handkerchief from his pocket, his wet face glistening in the bright sun.

Late in the afternoon of 7 September, in a clearing on Lüneburg Heath not far from the spot where a more famous British victory had earlier been recorded, Be Fair stood alone, the rest of Europe fanned out behind him. The loudspeaker announced his name, his new title and his nationality in three different languages. The British flag climbed the highest of the white poles as the band struck up the National Anthem. Be Fair stood like rock, four square, neck and head still and proud. I sat on his tight, short back, holding my whip vertically from my thigh in salute. Looking between his ears I saw the gold medal lying on a velvet covered table. I was not thinking about medals, instead I wondered if Be Fair had ever had ear-ache, like once I had had jaw-ache from smiling too widely. He always wore his ears so tightly pricked.

I wanted to ride Be Fair myself the two miles through the woods back to the stables because I wanted to savour every second with him. Those special moments evaporate all too soon. Instead I was scooped into the Press tent for a 'conference'. Joanna took him back. She did not ride, she led him because she wanted to talk to him and tell him that he was indeed 'The Greatest', all the way back to the stables.

The homeward ferry treated me to a night in the master-suite and a bunch of red carnations. Appleshaw had been raided by Karol and her three children, who did not like to think that we should return to an empty house. How sad that Erna had died six months earlier. She would have been ecstatic that her 'Be Fier' had won his title in her native land. Karol festooned the house with flowers. The children covered the outside of Be Fair's stable, windows and door with Christmas decorations. 'Welcome Home European Champion' was scribbled colourfully across a big white sheet of paper and more paper chains were pinned to the tack-room door.

'It's all cupboard love.' We prepare to leave Luhmühlen

Decorations welcome home the new European Champion

Wide Awake had been boarding out for the fortnight with Mary and Corny. He came home that afternoon with a plastic Union Jack hanging around his neck. It was suspended on blue ribbon with thirty-six small white labels stuck along its length, spelling out the message: W-E-L-L D-O-N-E T-H-E C-H-A-M-P-I-O-N-S B-E F-A-I-R A-N-D L-U-C-I-N-D-A.

Champagne flowed that evening and Be Fair was given his share much to his disgust. Anybody who could remember what we had been celebrating as we staggered to our beds early the next morning had done well.

Within the next few days both of us received a mass of lovely letters and telegrams. Nanny, who had never likened animals to humans and rarely went outside when she came to stay, wrote a brief congratulatory message in which she added 'Give Be Fair a pat from me. I talked to him before I left Appleshaw last time and I told him he could not retire until he had won a gold or even two; he listened very carefully.'

During the next week Be Fair wrote his thank you letters to all those who had helped him to his triumph, including an appallingly badly spelt one on a piece of Spillers Racehorse Nuts bag to 'Ladee Hooo ov Wylee'. Then he had to begin on his fan mail.

Champagne flowed most of that night. Daddy supports the gold medal

Meanwhile we collected together all the locals involved in his success, such as Mr Linsner, the blacksmith, and of course all the Cook family, and took them over to Fyfield to watch Luhmühlen restaged, courtesy of the BBC via Toby Balding's video-tape. Half way through, as the programme reached its climax coming towards showjumping day, the machine broke down, the tape was automatically rubbed off for ever and we all had to go home.

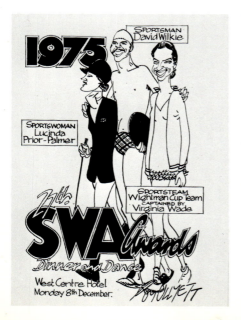

The Sports Writers' Association cartoonist had not missed much

Wakey had a lesson with Pat shortly afterwards. I hung the medal around my neck and buttoned my shirt over it, so that no one else sharing the lesson would see it. I wanted to show Pat the material proof of what her favourite boy had done, quietly at the end of the lesson when everyone had gone home. Unfortunately I did not notice it pop out between the buttons of my shirt. The others did and I nearly cried with embarrassment at being caught indulging.

Burghley Horse Trials took place the next week-end and I went to watch on foot. I met David and ran towards him, arms outstretched; both he and Pat had known Be Fair since his career began and through five long years they had encouraged and enlightened his rider with their patience and expertise. It was their victory as much as ours.

By the end of the month a horsey magazine had reproduced a fold out colour poster three feet square of Be Fair jumping out of the Luhmühlen water. The *Reiter Revue*, Germany's monthly *Horse and Hound*, portrayed across its front cover a coloured picture that probably best shows what Chris Collins meant when he wrote in an article later that year: 'Be Fair is the most elegant horse in eventing and his good looks clothe a core of steel.'

In early October Be Fair spent a week at Wembley appearing regularly once a night in the Horse of the Year Show's Personalities Parade. He was born to be on the stage and revelled in this nightly ritual.

He would enter the darkened arena and stand at the head of it between two huge pots of flowers. The spotlight flashed on to him as the commentator explained his credentials. As a horse who would never stand at the start and whose nerves had frequently ruined his dressage test, it would be reasonable to expect him to become impossible in such a situation. He never flinched, he stood stock still just as he had at the prize-giving in Luhmühlen, relishing every second. We cantered a few turns of the indoor stadium as the band played the theme tune that had been chosen for him, 'On top of the World'.

The show closed with a final cavalcade. Every competitor rode in and stood still, making a uniform pattern under the bright lights. The showjumpers formed a parallel line up the centre facing each other in a herringbone design. Be Fair was not amongst the 104 horses. He was hidden from sight behind a heavy crimson curtain and was caprioling in reverse down the entrance funnel. I had been asked to hold him back until the end and now I could not make him go forwards towards the curtain. I seriously doubted if I would ever persuade him through into the arena. When the horses inside the arena were sorted out and the atmosphere had once again become still and quiet, the heavy curtain drew slowly aside. Be Fair watched as it began to part and with barely a sign from me he forsook his Nastase habits and walked steadily towards the opening. Suddenly his behaviour was impeccable. Sombre and proud he marched slowly up the centre of the arena between the double line of showjumpers, coming to a halt in the centre under the big clock suspended high up in the roof.

He was announced with his new European title and was appointed the guest of honour in the final cavalcade. Standing erect and motionless we listened to the National Anthem.

'Personality of the Year': Wembley, 1975 (*Clive Hiles*)

12 Olympic Build-up

'The Year of the Horse' came onto BBC screens on the eve of the first day of 1976. It featured the two 1975 Equestrian European Champions, who consequently were the two hot favourites for Olympic Gold Medals. Showjumper Alwin Shockemohle's Warwick appeared with Be Fair.

The programme started in Germany with a fascinating insight into the home life of Alwin and his horses. It then returned to England and focused on Be Fair's country home. The leading sports' commentator, Raymond Brookes-Ward, introduced Be Fair.

'The thing that puts Be Fair and Lucinda out on their own is the way the horse is looked after. It's a family horse; Be Fair knows he's part of the family. He's the best looked after horse in the country. He knows that wherever he goes, the General in his old brown stockcoat, along with his wife, will always be there.'

A short interview was followed by films of Be Fair's achievements, Luhmühlen and Badminton, and of his fall there in 1974. My parents, I think, enjoyed another 'blubin', as we call them. I do not know for sure because I was abroad at the time. They did remember to tell me, however, what Simon had said at the end of the programme as he left the room. 'At least she was sober this time.' Once before at the end of 1972 I had been involved in the same programme, but on a very different theme. Eight riders were collected together and interviewed in the drawing-room of a country residence after a very good lunch indeed. We sat on sofas chatting merrily to the interviewer each with a glass of port near at hand.

Mine was the only one on the screen that was empty.

The Persians went to the expense of paying for my flight out to their country during the winter of 1975/76, in exchange for help with their showjumping and then proceeded to do the opposite to almost everything I suggested. Coupled with this frustration was the effect of the Muslim religion in which women hold no place of any consequence. I was no exception and found it impossible to try and organise anything. It was quite a relief to be home again by mid-January.

Be Fair had been assured of a place in the Olympic team and the selectors did not require to see him prove himself again at Badminton. All I had to do, they told me, was to keep him ticking over until July. That was seven months and they contained some of the least happy moments of our relationship. I tried my best not to become neurotic and told myself to treat him and our lives together as normally as I always had. It was impossible; Olympic fever had already struck and the Press were making the most of it. Throughout the winter and spring months the telephone was hot with calls requiring interviews, photographs or film sessions. Since Luhmühlen, Be Fair had learnt about cameras, he was no longer afraid. He loved to pose with his ears pricked. One of the photographers who had taken pictures of many horses told me how extraordinary he found it that when he worked with a celebrated horse it seemed to know that it was famous and would pose accordingly. I did not find it particularly extraordinary but then I suppose I had been under Be Fair's influence for too long. Annette Yarrow was sculpting £1,500 worth of bronze statue of Be Fair jumping into the Badminton Lake. It was to be raffled in aid of the British Olympic Equestrian Fund. While Be Fair was modelling during the early spring months, I was acting as technical advisor on a book called *Eventing*, which was to include a full chapter on the forthcoming Olympics and was scheduled for publication only three months after it. There was hardly a day when I did not either read a letter or a paper or talk to someone when the subject of the Olympics was not brought up.

Wide Awake was entered for Badminton. We had at last found the key to each other and the partnership was fast forming. He was coming into his own for he had won the Dutch International Three Day Event at Boekelo the previous October, and I had a 'feeling' about him and Badminton. Village Gossip, a horse who had shown much promise at Burghley in September, had been bought for me to ride. The *Horse and Hound* referred curtly and briefly to my fortune in having acquired yet another Three Day Event horse.

Be Fair was looking wonderfully strong and well as he came out in mid-March for his only outing that spring and won the Advanced One Day Event at Brigstock. Then to his amazement and before even the spring grass had come through, he was roughed off and turned out for a month's holiday. He knows so well when he is being made fit for an event and he thoroughly enjoys all the preparation. He will stand to be groomed with an expression of such contentment on his face that it reminds me of a poof at the hairdresser. He was very put out therefore, when all his beautifying came to an abrupt halt mid-way through the season and he was turned out to grass. Often he was naughty about being caught and if he felt like playing a game and wasting someone's time he would enjoy lungeing himself round the catcher in a perfect circle but never near enough to the human centre-point to be in danger of being grabbed. That spring he was so cross at having a holiday when he should have been going to Badminton that he made himself very awkward indeed. Once when we had all failed to catch him, Mummy resorted to crawling up to him on hands and knees with a carrot clenched between her teeth. He was sufficiently amazed by this apparition that he allowed himself to be caught, but it did not work the next time.

I was on a high; I could not help feeling height-sick when I looked down, there seemed to be a long, long way to fall.

The high continued however. Wide Awake led, following the cross-country at Badminton, by a similarly convincing margin as that of Be Fair three years previously. That evening, at the Badminton Ball, remarks and questions were flying about the dance floor. 'Which one will you ride in the Olympics?' 'God, she is so lucky – fancy having two horses as brilliant as Be Fair and Wide Awake to choose from for Montreal.'

I was in the other land again and I did not seriously digest what they were saying. I brushed it aside. I knew horses, I thought: one would go lame at the wrong moment. I doubted that I would have to make the choice between the two.

Barely twenty hours later, Wide Awake lay dying in the middle of the main arena at Badminton. He died from some kind of acute heart failure as he galloped his lap of honour. He died as we would all wish to go, in his moment of triumph.

Be Fair did not have much sleep for a time after Badminton. Late at night while all but the owls and foxes slept, I would pad out to his stable. He was nearly always lying down but he would stand up as I started to unbolt his door. He enjoyed being hugged and loved and would relax and become sloppy for a minute or so, sometimes for as long as five minutes. Then he would assert his individuality, pull back a little and shake his head once which meant that he had had enough. Those nights he never shook it. He stood still for ages, his head bent low as I looped my arms round his neck and buried my face in his mane. After some time I would leave him and walk down to say goodnight to Hysterical and Gossip and try to acclimatise myself to seeing Gossip's face looking over the door that for four years had framed another brown face. Invariably I returned to the house via Be Fair's stable; sometimes he had already gone back to bed. But he always got up and came over to give his comfort for as long as I wanted it. He never much liked Wide Awake but he must have been able to understand that I had lost something which carved deep into my happiness.

The temperature of Great Britain's Olympic fever was rising alarmingly fast. Montreal was suddenly only twelve weeks away.

The telephone spent much of its time off the hook for the Press had now a doubly juicy joint to hound and they do not all take hints easily. Charities wanted help and towards this chore I was bound to feel less rebellious. In June, I teetered down a catwalk in the grounds of the Tower of London, taking my part in the NSPCC fund-raising Fashion White Fantasia. Neither my dimensions nor my looks bore any resemblance to the skinny, sexy professional model and film star who swayed confidently down the catwalk, elegantly pivoting at the far end as they beamed into the surrounding audience, heads held aloft.

I had been disguised in a beautifully tailored, long-skirted white side-saddle outfit, complete with bun and white top-hat. Fortunately there was a veil of white netting for my face to hide behind. Waiting my turn in the wings I was enveloped by a similar feeling to the one I had had when I tried to do my first week-end job as a cook. I felt hideously inadequate, doing a task which I most certainly was not cut out to do. The complex about my elegance had started from a very early age when school friends wanted to nickname me Elephant, but found it was too much of a mouthful. I found myself trembling as I fumbled up the steps. I prayed that I would not perform a conventional Laurel and Hardy by making my entrance at speed, head-first, having tripped over my skirts on the way in.

I managed to walk slowly the whole way down to the other end, forcing my chin to hold my head up. As I went I silently cursed Be Fair; it was all his fault that I was doing this ridiculous act. I was wholly self-conscious and could only imagine how extraordinary I must look. On the return walk I made the fatal mistake of sparing one small glance at the front row. There I saw Princess Anne and Mark Phillips, glittering in full evening dress, sitting shaking with helpless laughter. That was too much for my self-control and I burst into convulsive giggles. I looked at the floor and somehow my feet took me out as the rest of me shook and shook.

The Olympic build-up was inevitable and I had expected the pressures, particularly after winning the European Championships. I was determined that it must not be allowed to affect me too much because I knew that if it did, I would inevitably let Be Fair down again.

For the fourth year in succession, Osberton was the scene of the final trial for the team, only this time it was Osberton with a difference. Owing to the Games being in July, the final trial had to take place in June, a month when there are no events and most horses are on holiday in Great Britain. Therefore a special competition was organised for the short-list alone.

Fashion White Fantasia. The marquee shook with laughter – it was all Be Fair's fault that I had to swagger down the cat-walk (*Desmond O'Neill*)

Front-page news

The 'programme' resembled a race-card as only eleven runners were involved. It was headed 'Pre-Olympic work-out'; underneath in small letters it read:

'The Competition: Please note that the selection committee may decide on the day that the work-out will not be run as a competition and some horses may be instructed to go slowly or omit some fences. It is stressed that "winning" this work-out is not an automatic passport into the final Olympic team. All gate money to the Equestrian Olympic Fund. Please keep dogs on leads.'

On 30 June Osberton Park welcomed any members of the public who might want to come and watch this inanimate performance. Most of the eleven contenders were highly disconsolate. The clay ground at Osberton has never retained much moisture in the summer, but during the tropical weather of 1976 it was baked so hard that deep cracks had appeared across the Park under the thin covering of grass. Be Fair's fore-legs looked still as good as new but I had taken even greater care of them since our fright two years ago. I realised they could not be as new as they looked, for he was thirteen and had completed eleven Three Day Events, not to mention numerous One Day Events, over all types of terrain during his seven years competitive career.

Most of us were loath to run our horses on the Osberton ground and protested in bulk that various particularly echoing sections of the course should be omitted. The selection committee discussed the protest and Colonel Bill gave us their reply 'If any of you want to be selected for the Olympic team you must complete the entire cross-country course.' There was a uniform groan to which he added 'The selection committee feel that if your horses are not sound enough to stand up to two miles on this ground, they certainly won't survive sixteen miles on possibly very similar ground in Canada.' That was their way of looking at it; but it did not coincide with the riders' view.

There was no option. The most cold-blooded contest I ever wish to take part in commenced at twelve noon the following day. Be Fair was first into the thankfully watered dressage arena where he produced a sparkling test for the second best mark, one point behind Persian Holiday and Mark Phillips. He jumped the showjumps as if his feet had two great corns in each of them. He slithered over every fence, not adding an inch more than necessary to its height, so the force of his descent onto the Tarmac-like ground would be minimal. He jumped fluently and quite happily across country but I did not enjoy my ride as I took him steadily and carefully round. There was no point in trying to beat the clock in order to win a prize – there were no prizes – nor was there any other incentive. It did not really matter how he went round. He was bound to be in the team; there was no reason for him not to be unless he injured himself by getting caught up in a fence, or unless this concrete going took its toll, or unless he put his foot down a rabbit hole, or ... painful anxieties were rife in my mind.

One by one each competitor returned to the shade and quiet refuge of the stable-yard. They flopped down onto an upturned bucket or one of the mounting blocks and stared at each other in silence. Eventually one would say 'Bloody awful, wasn't it? Christ, I hope they never put us through this waste of bloody time again.' As we waited each one watched his horse's legs like hawks eyeing a mouse, waiting to see if any warning signs of forthcoming trouble from strain or jarring would develop.

The months of tension which had been endured by everyone were coming to a head. Only one person was temporarily satisfied with how the head burst. Chris Collins and Smokey had little to lose and everything to gain. They went like scalded cats across country, caught up their dressage leeway and won the competition, work-out, team trial – call it what you like. They were not, however, picked for the Olympic team.

Once again we assembled for a week at Ascot. Princess Anne, Hugh Thomas, Richard Meade and myself, with Mark Phillips as reserve on both Favour and Persian Holiday. Jane Starkey lent her Topper Too to act as communal reserve horse and she was at Ascot and later at Bromont to look after him.

At last it was possible to relax a little. Only seven more days and we would be in Canada. We rode early every morning. The sun was merciless and David came nearly every day to help with Be Fair's dressage. During our final session he was riding him and Be Fair was being rather ornery, reckoning that he had been given too much discipline already that week. In retaliation he let out a particularly powerful capriole in one corner of the outdoor manège. David shot through the air and landed on his feet. Be Fair had never achieved such unexpected success before. I could not let either of them see how much I was laughing – very soon I thought, that horse will speak and the first word he says will be 'Shan't'.

In the afternoons we lounged by the swimming pool as Be Fair slept in the cool of his stable, his lower lip drooping contentedly. He knew he was nearing the greatest honour of his life – representing his country in the Olympic Games. Mary Browning, an artist very able to catch a likeness, came to sketch the heads of the seven Montreal-bound horses. A heart specialist came with a cardiograph to check the regularity of all the horses' hearts. Meanwhile the riders went to London to have final fittings, in the sweltering heat, of coats and breeches that, along with a riding hat from Locks, were generously donated to the lucky five by Messrs Huntsman and Sons. We had to spend one afternoon at the head-quarters of the British Olympic Association, a tiny first-floor office near King's Cross station, having fittings and trying on our Olympic kit. That *was* exciting. A lovely new set of luggage, stuffed with new clothes from socks, shoes and underwear to sun-hats, sunglasses and special Olympic T-shirts. It felt like Christmas and before we left I took all of it home to show Nanny, who was spending two weeks at Appleshaw.

At the end of the week, the lot fell to me to return to the steaming city of London and collect the finished garments from Huntsmans. I parked my sixteen-year-old green Mini on the yellow lines at the edge of Savile Row and went into the tailor's shop. Mr Lintott, who had been employed there long enough to know my father in 1930, helped me carry the beautiful sets of clothes out to the car. Red coats and white breeches for the men and blue coats and fawn breeches for the ladies. The special Olympic buttons and the new breast-pocket Union Jack showed clearly through the protective polythene layering which stuck to our arms in the heat as we carried them

Mary Browning's superb, life-like portraits of the seven horses bound for Montreal

across the street to the car. The outfits were works of art. I do not think Mr Lintott appreciated laying them in the far from pristine seat of my dilapidated Mini, with Oliver in the passenger seat, eyeing the new 'cushions', long pink tongue hanging out as he panted for extra air. After I had crawled backwards out of the Mini, I stood up, thanked Mr Lintott, and said goodbye. I stooped down, sank into the sticky driver's seat and slammed the door. The window, complete with frame, fell out onto the pavement. I was as horrified as Mr Lintott because I knew I had another errand to do, which would entail leaving hundreds of pounds worth of new tailored hunting clothes in a car without a window.

I wanted to put Be Fair's thick protective leg-bandages on him myself before his long flight across the Atlantic and rose at 3.00 in the morning to do so. At 4.00 am dawn was just beginning to make an impression on night as all the horses were loaded into the horse-box that was to take them to Gatwick. Or all but one were loaded. Be Fair stood at the bottom of the ramp, ears pricked, nose stuck out with that stubborn, arrogant look on his face. Joanna was leading him. She did not worry, she knew Be Fair. She did not bother to try to persuade him further. Two lungeing reins were promptly found and attached to the horse-box, either side of the ramp. I did not even have to bend down to pick either of them up before he stepped sedately onto the ramp and walked unhurriedly into his stall in the horse-box. Often he felt like making his presence felt for a few minutes, and would refuse to go up a ramp until someone went to the extra trouble of finding, bringing and attaching the two reins. One rein was not good enough for him. He rarely gave anyone the chance to pick them up let alone close them behind his quarters before he would walk unconcerned and quietly triumphant into the horse-box.

The tail lights of the two lorries flickered and bumped up the rutty drive towards the road. It was 4.15 in the morning. Seven years ago it probably would have been 6.15 am before Be Fair would have agreed to load and let them depart. Progress, I thought to myself, progress.

13 Real Life

The horses had already arrived by the time our Jumbo Jet screamed to a standstill outside the Montreal International Air Terminal.

The airport was festooned with every sort of reminder of why we had come. A man in a bright red suit and multi-coloured striped tie came to meet us and lead us through customs. I thought he must be a little strange to wear such effeminate clothes, but then I saw the female edition and slowly began to realise that this crisp, sunny colour scheme, soon to become so familiar, was worn by all the official Olympic hosts and hostesses.

A police escort of two cars and a helicopter accompanied the coach that took us half an hour up the freeway to Bromont, high in the mountains of a winter ski-resort and site of the 1976 Equestrian Olympic Games. No coach load of competitors, no matter what their nationality, was allowed to make an excursion without a helicopter escort. The nightmare of the murdered Israelis in Munich had laid a heavy responsibility on the Canadian authorities.

The sky was very dark and rain drizzled as we disembarked in front of a new wooden pavilion surrounded by particularly bright green grass. Everything everywhere, seemed to be new and especially built for the Games. We tried to walk across the grass towards the entrance of the pavilion but our feet sank into the soft, oozing mud hidden beneath the emerald shoots. That was pleasantly surprising for we had thought the ground in Canada would be like that at Osberton.

We were not allowed to go to the stables until we had obtained our identity cards. For two hours we filled in forms and waited in queues. Armed police, some determined to understand only their native French, others more hospitable, took their time in officially enlisting each one of us as a competitor at the Olympic Games. It struck me that the security would have to be treated with a determined good humour or it would begin to play on everyone's fraying nerves. Russia seemed nearly a free country by comparison.

Those I.D. cards were vital, as many were to learn to their inconvenience. Before the English arrived, an Australian rider had already become so incensed one night when he was not allowed back into the 'Olympic Village' to go to his own bed that he had a punch-up with one of the policemen on guard at the entrance. He had left his I.D. card the other side of the gates actually in his own bedroom. These plastic-covered cards displaying a passport-sized photograph of the bearer were worn on a white nylon string around the neck all the time – even in bed, especially if the wearer was destined to be up early and therefore apt to forget to put them on.

The security was indeed fantastic. The brand new series of semi-detached houses in the village were enclosed by twelve feet of barb-topped wire mesh. Entrance into either the village or the pavilion, which housed the catering and recreation areas, could be made only by passing through one single narrow channel between electric eyes that squawked rudely if anyone had absentmindedly forgotten to leave their hand grenade outside.

The stables were two miles from the village at the end of the route of a half hourly shuttle bus service. I never did discover the correct departure times of this bus, and once I decided not to wait for it but to walk back to the village. I took a short cut along the single railway track which ran nearby and decided to run its length to improve my fitness. I wore a pair of shorts, the blue Olympic suede gym shoes and my Great Britain track-suit top. My I.D. card flapped up hitting me in the face at every stride. I swung it round so that it hit me on the back of the head instead. Ambling down the track towards me came one of the hundreds of armed policemen that were not only huddled around the village and stables but also scattered liberally across the mountainside. This one stopped me forcefully as I trotted gaily past holding my I.D. out towards him in one hand. I told him in my best bad French that I could not stop or it would ruin my training. That did not impress him in the least. He spent at least thirty seconds studying my card as if he had never seen one before and then unsheathed his walky-talky and tuned in to his boss. Two long minutes later he reluctantly let me go but told me to stick to the roads in future. I told Richard the story and on his next run he obeyed and stuck to the roads. He was stopped and told not to run but to walk. Things did improve however, as the teething problems and the jitters of the security force decreased. They soon became accustomed to the strange habits of horse riders. Runs were no longer prohibited, provided the roads were used and the I.D. card was not zipped up inside the track-suit or obscured in any other way.

The horses had good indoor wooden stables. Nearly every country was allotted a separate block to itself. Each block was cut into the side of the mountain, as were most of the seventeen specially sanded and drained practice areas. From a distance the complex resembled an Italian vineyard.

The bright green grass surrounding everything was poisonous. Be Fair could not understand, and nor could we, why it had been necessary to spray it with a deadly gas to make it grow greener quicker. The facilities for the horses' welfare and training were the most exotic I had ever seen. In an area near the stables there were communal horse showers: open-air stalls, each with hot and cold pressure hoses. A huge sack of carrots was given to each stable block whenever required. Freezer chests stood in every block. One held ice-creams and ice lollies, the other soft fizzy drinks and in time a good deal of Peter Scott-Dunn's veterinary potions, when he discovered the freezer's location. Every dressage arena looked well enough equipped, with its beautiful white boards and black lettering, to have been the Olympic arena itself. Any prepared area that was bigger than a dressage arena was filled with new sets of showjumps. Galloping and cantering, ad infinitum, was allowed around the man-made sanded track, which lay in the bottom of the valley and formed the official steeplechase course, its mile length encircling a great lake. The authorities told us with pride that they had imported a pair of the rare Canada Geese to the lake. They felt that the birds symbolized the 1976 Olympics.

Unlike the massive, sardine packed Olympic Village in the city of Montreal, our 'village' accommodation was quite adequate. There were two in each bedroom, unless you had the good fortune to have been allotted the dining-room or the sitting room, in which case you were on your own. These semi-detached houses were modern and had no doors downstairs. I used to wake up in my dining-room, staring at the gas cooker, or I was woken up by someone delivering a parcel in the hall, about six feet from my nose. The pavilion provided plenty of good food and fresh fruit, offering a wide choice, and although mass produced it never became repetitive. On the other side of the screens at the end of the dining-room was the badminton court, surrounded by ping-pong tables; these were dominated mostly by sadistic Russians, who would stand by their tables, a bat in each hand, offering one to a would-be opponent. Their skill in slicing and cutting the ball and finishing off a victim in under two minutes revealed to me what a Russian man must do with those long dull evenings we had experienced in Kiev.

Be Fair and I were both thoroughly content. For the

first time since I had returned from Persia I was able to relax properly and enjoy his company. If anything went wrong now, well, too bad, at least we were here, loving and living this Martian Olympic existence. Anyway I did not think anything would go wrong. I felt as positive and as confident as I dared and I looked forward to the competition. For two whole weeks we were free of any responsibilities save one.

Be Fair was enjoying the rides on the mountains and his back muscles negotiated the steep climbs with more ease than I had expected. A gentle mountain breeze and the sun beating down combined to create a perfect climate and the conditions had become good underfoot. The Olympics were fun.

In a situation as important as this with such superb facilities, the temptation is to overtrain a horse in the last ten days. Everyone seemed to be galloping everywhere, every day. Those that were not normally partial to dressage were lured into one of the exotic arenas every day, sometimes even twice a day.

Colonel Bill and Peter Scott-Dunn watched their team each day at work but they did not see much of Be Fair down by the Canada Geese. For two years I had pursued my 'tribal rites' and at Luhmühlen the year before both Colonel Bill and Peter had remarked on Be Fair's superlative condition. But this was the Olympics. The course was going to be mountainous and very arduous. Was I quite sure that Be Fair was going to be fit enough? Was he really having enough work?

I was quite sure. Be Fair was very fit, his legs hard and clean, and what was just as important he was fit and ready in his mind. He was happy, gay and keen. These last three things were more important for him than anything else. He was quick to switch off and become stale if he was worked too much in the few weeks preceding a big competition.

To the outside world the English only had the Ameri-

Two faces from the scrapbook: Col. Bill Lithgow and Peter Scott-Dunn

cans to beat. All the other ten nations were classed as 'also ran'. It would be a tough fight to beat the reigning world champions but, spurred on by tremendous positive thought and leadership from the invincible Colonel Bill, we all thought we could and hoped that we would.

I discussed training with Bruce Davidson one day, when I met him riding through the woods in the valley of Bromont. He was always genuine with his help. Once I asked him why he helped the opposition.

'Because,' he replied, 'if I win I wanna know I won 'cos I was the best, not 'cos I had a better method.' I explained that I was still having trouble convincing people of the value of interval training and that very few riders in England had wanted to experiment with it. He smiled at me and said nothing, but his expression said it all. How will the British rebuild their success when so many of them will not open their minds, admit that they are not always the wisest, and sometimes be prepared to change their ways?

Thanking Bruce again for the counsel he had always been happy to give me, I told him that in Bromont

219

interval training was probably proving my greatest asset. With the prospect of the cross-country drawing near, the inevitable panic had set in. Most asked themselves whether or not their particular horse was as fit as he could possibly be for the Olympic Games. They could never be certain of the answer and many, therefore, felt it best to undertake last minute, emergency canter and fast work – just in case. My programme was charted on paper. It was similar to previous charts, whose worth I had already proved to myself. Time and again during a Three Day Event, genuine people had given me great pleasure by saying my horse looked the fittest. Both at Luhmühlen, then with Wide Awake at Boekelo and Badminton, their judgement had been confirmed. I was confident therefore and easily able to hold off the panic, but only because I had the evidence and did not have to rely solely on using my ears and eyes to gauge the fitness of my horse. Bruce, I think, realised the depth of my gratitude.

A week after our arrival and five days before the cross-country day, Be Fair encircled the geese for the first time on his final leg of interval training. He cantered 10 (3) 10 (3) $4\frac{1}{2}$ with a six furlong gallop at three-quarter speed to finish. I hoped the party of British team officials who stood watching felt happier. I certainly was delighted with how my horse had felt on his pre-Olympic workout.

Despite the changes in my methods of fitness-training, I had still no better method to prepare Be Fair for the dressage than that which I had always used. He still had to be out of his stable for long periods of time before his test. My principal objective was to prevent him blowing up and becoming overwrought when he entered the taut atmosphere of an arena surrounded by a multitude of spectators. I knew it was no use working him into the ground for he was far too fit ever to become tired doing four hours of dressage and he would be sure to become ornery instead. Somehow I had to prevent him exploding by working not on his physical state but on his mental attitude.

Joanna plaited him on the morning of his test and I spent two hours walking him about in the area of the stadium. Be Fair was never able to see the arena for it was enclosed on two sides by steep hills, and on the other two by vast scoreboards and a grandstand. I gave him his pre-cross-country pipe opener, a sharp two furlong gallop on the steeplechase track nearby and then worked him with a low, stretched-out neck for three-quarters of an hour's trot and canter until he felt thoroughly relaxed and was working kindly.

We returned to the stables and I ordered that Be Fair be left in peace for an hour, with a small lunch and his net of soaked hay. He was supposed to imagine that he had finished the day's work, relax and fill some of his tummy with food. Joanna knew that he would roll and was furious that she had had to plait him beforehand, for the new tacky white shavings would become entwined in his plaits and make him look a mess. She had pleaded with me to let her plait him later after his lunch instead of in the early morning. She lost her cause. Be Fair must be left alone to relax for an hour between his morning work and his test. But she was absolutely right, he did roll. We had allowed time for it though. During the final fifteen minutes when he was groomed and tacked up ready for his test, my mother and father descended on his neck and carefully disentangled each separate shaving which had caught itself in the hairs of his plaits.

The sun shone out of a brilliant blue sky reflecting off my high black boots and black top-hat, which shone like glass after my father had given its silk covering a polish with the stout that he had brought with him specially from England. One hour and five minutes after he had left the stables for the second time that day, Be Fair trotted down the funnel and into the Garden of Eden,

– the Olympic arena. 'Smile,' Ronnie Masserella, the showjumping chef d'équipe, kept his promise to make me laugh and relax as I was about to begin my dressage. It worked. On a loose rein I let Be Fair look about him and absorb his surroundings during the two minutes grace each competitor is allowed before his test commences. By each marker there were pots overflowing with flowers and shrubs in the Olympic colours. Here and there amidst beds of wallflowers and the bright unrealistic green of the grass, a large rock lay ominously crouching as if it were a large lion waiting to spring. I wondered what Be Fair would think of these strange surroundings; whether or not he would decide it was best to take cover from such monsters. I had no idea if he would rise to the occasion in my sense of the word, or use it as an audition for Chipperfield's Circus.

As we waited for the arena party to finish smoothing out every footfall in the sand that had been left by the Australian Bill Roycroft, veteran of five Olympics, I slowed Be Fair to a walk.

He had sensed the importance of the occasion but with his extraordinary intelligence he also knew what that occasion demanded. Having had his look around, I felt him untense his tight muscles and so mine relaxed too. I allowed him to walk and stretch his neck and head to confirm in his mind that this was the mental approach we intended to preserve throughout the next eight minutes.

He performed quite beautifully. He did not make a semblance of a mistake, either in the various movements or in the execution of them. He was submissive and attentive and his ears were pricked throughout. Maybe he felt that there were enough people watching to make it worthwhile doing his very best. Nonetheless, as he turned for the final time up the centre line he was unable to resist bursting into an extravagant extended trot towards the judges, accidently-on-purpose misunderstanding my aid which had asked him for canter. It made me

The Montreal Olympics: We finish our dressage test, one of the best Be Fair has ever done (*L. B. van der Slikke*)

laugh so much as he did it that I could not find the strength to pull him back and try again until he was past the centre marker at X. After managing only four strides of canter he reached the point of halt and salute. He stopped and stood proudly, staring at the judges inside their glass boxes, as if to ensure that he had transfixed them with the magic of his presence.

The British camp rejoiced in Be Fair; he was well in front of any of the other British horses and lay fifth in the world. Karl Shultz and Madrigal, however, were twenty-five marks in front of him. World champions Bruce Davidson and Irish Cap were ten marks in front and an unheard-of young American riding a mare called Ballycor, and the great Mike Plumb on Better and Better were only a few marks behind us.

Hans Winkler, showjumping in his sixth Olympics, was reasonably complimentary about our dressage test. Only reasonably, not ecstatically complimentary, and in the back of my mind I knew why. Be Fair had left the arena that afternoon giving me the feeling that we had produced the best test we were capable of together. I felt, however, that he was capable of much, much better but I did not know how to produce it. This void of expertise, coupled with the infinitely better marks of the Germans, marked the moment when two and two began to make four in my mind and the seeds of the future were sown. Winkler looked at me through the gold-rimmed spectacles he always wore, and asked how I thought the cross-country course would ride. He suffered a few moments of my furrowed brow and worried remarks and then cut in with:

'Aah, zis is not at all like zee girl I knew two years ago in Warendorf. Vat is viz you, viz all zis fussing? Ze reason you 'ave ever been successful is because of your "take it as it comes" attitude, now you behave like an old, vot shall I say, an old grandmozzer? Be careful Luzinda, it is zese traps vich many fall into ven zey reach ze very top, zat is how zey fall down zo quick.'

He turned and walked away. I watched as the short stocky back-view, topped by black but thinning hair, dissolved into the milling crowd. What wisdom. How well he understood that the greatest part of riding lay in the mind. He must know his own mind extremely well, for he had stayed at the top for nearly a quarter of a century.

The results following the dressage were much as we had expected. The Germans led, followed by the Americans and then the British, and that night at the final team briefing, British morale ran high. There was a wonderful team spirit amongst us. The glint of battle shone in every eye as we each discussed our final plan of attack on the forthcoming speed and endurance test. 'It is the gold medal we are here to win and nothing less,' echoed Colonel Bill as he bade us goodnight and sweet dreams.

Be Fair was the team's strong man. He was in place number four and we felt well able to shoulder our responsibilities. I slept soundly for over eight hours.

I awoke on cross-country morning at 8.10 am. No one had found time to attend to such detail as curtains in the 'village' quarters and immediately I could see through the dining-room windows that the dark sky was heavy with rain.

How depressing. The sun makes me feel bold and happy, as I had felt at the previous night's briefing. It was almost an anticlimax, as if everything had suddenly gone wrong, and yet it was only a change of weather. I lay in bed for a while, wondering how long I would be able to trick myself into staying relaxed this time and musing over the fact that poor Hugh Thomas on Playamar would already be on Phase A. Soon they would be thundering twice round the geese in the valley, or maybe sploshing round. On closer inspection it became evident that rain had been falling all night. I could do nothing to help Hugh's effort as number one team trail blazer and I do not like walking round the course the morning of the cross-country, preferring to conserve every ounce of energy. I had decided, therefore, to have a leisurely breakfast reading the Canadian papers to kid myself for as long as I could that it was of no consequence that Be Fair and I would be setting out at 1.34 that afternoon to face together the greatest challenge of our lives.

Breakfast was very leisurely and strength-giving. Bacon, eggs and sausages were consumed but I do not remember what news the papers held.

My energy-saving routine was forced to deviate somewhat when I found it was infinitely less frustrating and certainly quicker to walk up to the stables instead of sitting restlessly in the bus, queuing with coaches and cars strung for miles along the approach road. Many others coming to the same conclusion abandoned their transport and the crush of people surging along either side of the road was reminiscent of shopping in Oxford Street.

Eventually, a little harrassed at the thought of such an unnecessary waste of carefully conserved strength, I climbed the final steep slope leading to the British stables and went in to have a word with Be Fair. I let myself quietly into his stable, planted a good morning kiss on the soft velvet nose and quickly withdrew. He was resting in the corner of his stable and he had not enjoyed being disturbed. He was trying to relax and had on the familiar sick face that he wears prior to cross-country. Evidently he was taking his morning as seriously as I was taking mine, except he had not felt breakfast to be a necessary preliminary.

Only a few minutes later his peace was disturbed. A mud-spattered and bedraggled Playamar was led through the door of the block, his flanks heaving and a tense, worried look on his face. Something prevented me asking his groom, Margaret, how he had fared. I had a sinking notion all was not well. The next moment Hugh walked into the block. He looked very wet; no wonder, it was raining. But no, he looked too wet just for rain. There was no weed hanging off him but I was fairly certain he must have fallen in the Lake.

'Bloody deep, Lucinda. You want to watch it. I might have gone a bit fast, I don't know – the old boy just folded up in the water as he landed over the drop. It rides well though, the rest of the course, you'll be all right.' He added this as an afterthought to encourage his team-mate. Worse was to come.

In the next half hour it became clear that poor Playamar had broken down badly on one of his fore-legs and would be unable to complete the competition the next day. Poor Hugh, he had come second to Wide Awake at Badminton that year and for four years he had steered everything towards Montreal. Now look what had befallen both of them.

The feeling of anticlimax was growing fast. I was gloomy and less enthusiastic about the task ahead. Things were not unfolding quite as we had anticipated in our exercise of positive thought.

Resignedly I began to change into my breeches and boots while Jo finished plaiting Be Fair. I heard a commotion outside the tack-room, and hopped to the door with one boot on and one bare foot. Princess Anne was standing in the passage-way, Mark inconspicuously supporting her. She looked wet and dazed.

'Oh God,' I thought, 'I can't bear it, another one, another disaster.' I looked at her breeches – they were muddy with grey-green stains streaked across them. She had not fallen in the water, she was not quite wet enough, but she must have come down somewhere. A mud-splattered Goodwill clip-clopped through the entrance and was led down the passage to his stable. At least he looked in better shape than Playamar had when he came back.

Great Britain's number two came into the tack-room and nodded at me. I had to know what had happened to her. It might be a vital piece of information that I should digest, and soon I would be gone to start on Phase A myself. I felt it inhuman to ask but this was important business. This was the Olympics, we were both members of the same British team, and it was not the time to play the tactful subject. I braved the consequences. I was not sure what the reply would be but I certainly did not expect to hear what I did.

'I'm terribly sorry, I can't remember a single thing after fence 18.'

I worked out which was fence 18 and presumed with some puzzlement that she must have fallen at the following one, an innocuous zig-zag rails over a ditch. Five minutes later Princess Anne returned to the tack-room.

'I've remembered something,' she said. 'I jumped fence 19 on the right and Goodwill never took off. He seemed to get stuck in the mud, or slipped or something.' The weather must have been altering conditions rapidly.

'Thanks,' I said. 'Anything else? How did the rest ride?'

'I can't remember a thing about it.'

Be Fair nearly never started the Olympic Games. He would not allow us to put his saddle on. Jo was walking him round at the start of Phase A, as I weighed-in. Every five minutes a vulgar bleeper, which Be Fair had already met at Luhmühlen, belched out the countdown for every competitor: five low staccato tones followed by a high prolonged note which meant 'Go' in whatever language you happened to speak, and that included Be Fair's. He wheeled round in lightning turns, lifting Jo off her tiny feet as he backed away, kicking and bucking with anticipation and excitement. He could not regain his composure long enough to enable us to put the saddle on, let alone do up the girths. As Jo flew once more through the air, I failed to see any amusement in the situation and then my mother and father moved in to help.

We all knew Be Fair when he was like this; we all knew how impossible he was to deal with. My father was on one side and I was on the other whilst Jo and my mother tried to anchor him in front. With foot work that would impress a tap-dancer, especially from someone of seventy-three, Daddy and I managed to strap the saddle in place and I was quickly legged up. I could not face the possibility of him escaping with Joanna bobbing along at the end of the reins, making no more impression on him than a balloon would on the sea. Once I was on him he was better for a few minutes. No doubt the tension about him had slackened too. Although my parents, Jo and I had not said it, each one of us was seriously worried that we might never manage to get the saddle on in time for his start.

The starter bleeped at Bill Roycroft in Australian and Be Fair became incensed. He had watched and waited for long enough. Five jiggery-pokery minutes later we started on our first phase of the Speed and Endurance Test of the 1976 Olympic Games.

Be Fair and I were alone now; I smiled to myself. It was him and me against the world and the rain had ceased. The disaster stories that had dripped into the stables so short a time ago seemed far away now. Be Fair relaxed into his energy-saving, lollopy canter that he reserved especially for roads and tracks. I marvelled at him once again. It had taken him no more than a quarter of a kilometre to stop fighting for his head and to realise that this was Phase A and he had not yet reached either the steeplechase or the cross-country course.

The start of Phase B had been carefully paced out and timed by my father, and Jo duly delivered Be Fair and me into the start box on the final low tone of the bleeper. He found the steeplechase hard work, two miles in soft, newly laid sand which had sucked in fifteen hours of continuous rain. In places it was sinking half way up his leg bandages. I tried to keep off the beaten track but it was equally holding everywhere. Despite the conditions Be Fair jumped and galloped with his usual tremendous power and zest. I never felt him struggling as I had feared he might but the deep going obviously slowed his speed. Splattering through the finish, wet sand flying into the faces of the time-keepers, I glanced at my own watch and realised that he had clocked exactly five minutes – one second more and he would have had 0.8 of a time-fault. Such accurate judgement was only luck, for I had aimed to be twelve seconds under the time.

We were happy. Alone we scaled the quiet undulations of the wooded foothills. I felt things were running our way. Be Fair must have felt the same; he had never before executed Phase C so effortlessly and maintained quite such peace of mind and relaxation of body. I had been worried about Phase C because I knew he found hills particularly hard work and I had feared that nine kilometres of mountaineering might take the edge off him. But my fears proved groundless and I started to sing. It was my own personal yoga and, provided there was no one else to hear, it kept my nerves in harmony.

There was nothing dramatically disheartening to be learnt from the briefing after our arrival in the box. I already knew the worst. Richard Meade was there brimming as usual with welcome confidence. In his masterly fashion he had persuaded the green, gangling eight-year-old, Jacob Jones, to jump round the cross-country course clear and fast. Surely, despite a less-masterly jockey but as a horse of infinitely more experience, Be Fair could do likewise? Our orders were straightforward. Colonel Bill had decided that there was no point in sending me round to play safe, although now only two out of the first three members of the team remained. He walked with me as I went over to mount Be Fair and said in a quiet and low-toned voice:

'This is a chance in a lifetime – you might never be in this position again. Go out there and *Go* for that individual gold medal.' I felt as confident as my pre-cross-country nerves would allow. On my instructions Jo released Be Fair into the start box a second too early. In any other competition in the world I believe I would have escaped judgement. But the Olympics is the world's top competition and the world's top judges are there. Be Fair shot across the start line as the final low toned note of the start died. As the prolonged high note began my leg was opposite the start flag. A Canadian voice bellowed 'False Start, False Start.'

I pulled Be Fair up from his flight, returned a few yards back to behind the line and recommenced. For a brief moment I thought that those few seconds wasted might make a vital difference to the result. Then, because I was so certain of Be Fair's ability and speed and confident in what lay ahead, I felt that we would be able to make up the lost time and I never gave another thought to our false start.

The cross-country day is featured in detail in the Olympic Three Day Event film. Many who have watched it have told me that there was only one other horse in the whole of the Olympic Games whose round across country could be compared with Be Fair's.

He was at his best and most inspired. He had been since he entered the dressage arena the previous day. From start to finish he did not give me one moment of concern. The course was not as huge and impressive as Badminton, but it was fiddly and twisted up and down steep gradients. In places the going was deep, in others it was good. A course of that description would not normally have been one that Be Fair particularly enjoyed and he would usually start to jump accordingly. At Bromont he did not enjoy the false bits of ground but that was all, for he relished his jumping. Shortly before the lake I felt him tire a little and as he pulled his feet out of another boggy patch I patted him and spoke to him, encouraging him to keep up his spirits. His ears pricked up tighter and he jumped the next fence with his accustomed ease and care and then flowed over the three parts forming the lake fence as if he were a piece of silk running uninterruptedly through a sewing machine. The cheers he received as he jumped clear of the lake were so tumultuous that his fire was re-fuelled for the remainder of the course. On top of the following hill a great roar arose from the British contingent. Be Fair responded with another surge of propulsion as he cleared the soft

Be Fair, looking intelligent and alert, sums up the next fence. Montreal Olympics (*Hugo M. Czerny*)

brush fence by six inches.

The penultimate fence consisted of three big sleeper steps rising in tiers, followed by a vertical fall and a sharp turn over a log-pile at the base of the bank. This fence had caused me concern when I walked the course. I felt sure that after all the hills and twists and turns Be Fair would be tiring by then. However, he pinged up each step, hesitated momentarily at the summit as he balanced himself, measured up the log-pile at the base and slid neatly down the bank, one and a half strides and over the logs. He felt as if he would go on forever. He stood back at the last fence, a miserable little hayfeeder at the top of a long incline. He had done it, he had given the round of his life when we wanted it most – how incredible, how lucky I was. As he landed I turned left-handed and kicked for the finish only fifty yards away.

His assessment is correct; he launches himself over the Trakhener (*Hugo M. Czerny*)

And then it happened. I had felt nothing and was only vaguely aware of wondering why he had not increased his speed between the turn and the finish. Then we were already through the posts and pulling up. Something felt weird underneath me. He was hopping behind, holding his off-hind leg in the air every other stride. I hoped that he had simply knocked himself on the shin as he pulled up; he was a great hypochondriac and often held a leg up if he had given it a blow.

It was quickly apparent that hypochondria was not to blame. Something was very definitely amiss. I had no idea what it could be. Normally the weighing-in scales are at the finish but in Bromont they were over 200 yards away at the end of a roped-in channel of rough and bumpy ground. I could not dismount before the weighing-in steward ordered or I would automatically eliminate myself and thereby the entire British team. Be Fair hurried along the channel in an uncontrolled walk as if he was trying to escape from something. I sat there unable to do more than try to contain him and keep him slow. Meanwhile my eyes scanned the box area looking desperately for Peter Scott-Dunn.

An agonising forty-five seconds later we arrived. Be Fair halted, the stewards held him and told me to dismount. I went round his back legs. I could not see anything wrong anywhere. Then a dreadful thought struck me. He had been staggering – Wide Awake staggered too – was Be Fair having heart failure, was he about to collapse? Peter had arrived. He assured me in his confident manner that Be Fair was not about to collapse.

I unsaddled him and quickly weighed-in. Someone took the saddle off me, I do not know who and once again I studied Be Fair's back leg. I could see nothing. I looked up at Peter.

'What's happened?' I asked.

'He's done a Columbus.'

It took a whole forty minutes to produce the second horse ambulance, the first being already in use. During that time the situation grew grimmer. Be Fair felt his hind leg suddenly unable to support him as the Achilles' tendon wobbled from side to side instead of up and down the back of his hock. He panicked and plunged forwards, kicking violently with his off-hind trying to rid himself of the pain. It became worse and he panicked more. The reserve rider, Mark Phillips, was already helping me to restrain him and then, as he ploughed through someone's store of equipment scattering buckets, towels and water carriers, I had to relinquish my hold to two more strong men: Dick Stillwell and Mike Bullen. When he was still I stood with him and talked to him, and I noticed that his breathing was already nearing its normal rate. He must have been very fit. I spared a thought of thanks to Bruce and his system and hoped that he would win a medal now that Be Fair could not.

Such an injury as this is indeed a rarity and Peter could not believe that it had happened to both Columbus and Be Fair at the end of important competitions within two years. I knew that the 'one chance in a lifetime' that Colonel Bill had referred to was gone forever but I did not care. It was Be Fair whom I wanted to win a medal, not myself. In comparison to this hideous outcome, its importance as far as I was concerned seemed no greater than its worth – a small, round, shiny piece of tin dangling from a nylon ribbon.

The only place the injury could have possibly occurred was on the turn across the face of the hill between the last fence and the finish. How ironic.

'It must be meant,' I kept repeating to myself, 'it must be meant. One day I'll understand why it had to happen.'

Be Fair had unleashed more depth of talent and skill than ever before at a moment when it mattered most. He had indeed shown the world that he was the greatest. After all, it is the manner of achieving which matters, and not the material achievement itself. I stepped quickly out of his path. Another spell of panic as he tried in vain to free himself from this strange and terrifying feeling sent him surging forwards thrashing his hind-legs through the air with the velocity of a slave driver's whip.

Would they decide it was best to put him down? It was unthinkable, but the next moment I found myself almost wishing they would – rather that fate, which I had dreaded for so many years, than a continuation of the dreadful pain he must be suffering.

Meanwhile Daddy waited and waited to receive Be

Fair at the compulsory dope-test centre. Eventually he asked some passing Canadians if the chestnut horse from Great Britain was on his way up.

'Oh – ya' mean Be Fair, that horse with the look of eagles? Oh gee – he can't move from the finish, he's hurt bad, real bad.'

With the aid of a tranquilliser, Be Fair was eventually loaded into a trailer, whose towing car promptly became stuck and had to be pulled out of the mud by an army lorry. I walked up to the stables keeping pace with the slow moving trailer, my hand on the handle of the passenger door in case Mark and Mike needed an escape hatch should Be Fair panic inside the trailer.

Shavings were quickly spread over the concrete passage-way leading into Be Fair's stable. Ears drooping from the effect of the tranquilliser, he hopped in a series of individual efforts along the ten yards of covered passage to his stable. Every so often he would kick out violently with the one back leg but he still had enough instinct despite his worry not to hit the wooden wall. The force produced by his kick would have sent his foot straight through the planking. When he settled a little more, Peter, Joanna and I wound a big crêpe bandage round his hock to help support him. The hock had already began to blow up and by then was the size of a tennis ball. No one could do anything for him.

Peter assured me that in a day or two Be Fair would become accustomed to the new feeling and start to put a little weight on the leg. Meanwhile we must make him as happy as we could and try to keep his kidneys clear as he would not be able to stretch out to pee for a time. Joanna faced the situation with the same courage that she showed when her father died suddenly nine months later.

The team ate a quiet, civilised dinner in a near-by Swiss-style hotel where the Russells and several others were staying. After we had eaten we watched the news on the hotel television. A bright-faced female newscaster read out that the US team were leading in the Three Day Event at Bromont and the British team were lying second. Individually, Karl Shultz and Madrigal of Germany were still in the lead. America's favourite, World Champion Bruce Davidson, had lost his chance when he was submerged like many others before him in the lake. She put on a sombre face, looked me straight in the eye and said, 'Other misfortunes occurred during the day, but notably to Great Britain. Lucinda Prior-Palmer's Be Fair slipped an Achilles' tendon and will never compete again . . .' Richard shoved a glass of wine into my hand and told me to drink it. I smiled into the glass, there was nothing else to do except drink it.

In the village later that evening Hugh, despite his misfortunes a tower of strength, lent me a book. Normally I never seem to read but my mind needed an instant distraction. I took the book with me to breakfast the following morning and read it. I took it when I went to see Be Fair and sat on the concrete, leaning against the outside of his stable and read it. Wherever I went I took it and if I had to stop I started to read. I cannot remember what the book was called and I certainly do not recall what it was about – but I read it – I could not risk thinking just yet.

My parents and I went to watch the vets' inspection. The British team was officially rubbed off the scoreboard as only two British horses came up before the panel for inspection. They both looked radiant and passed easily. The German team vet sitting on the grass in front of me, watching, turned and said unexpectedly but simply, 'What a pity – but you know in Germany we find this accident happens to horses that have been on Butazolidin a long time.'

Be Fair had never lived on Bute. All my horses start on a course of this widely used and legalised pain reliever the day before every Three Day Event. This is to ensure that a superficial bang sustained across country will not render them unsound at the vets' inspection and in the showjumping on the following day. I had had enough of this Bute business. In the months following Badminton, newspapers from all over the world had, in their ignorance, accused me of killing Wide Awake by using Bute and now I could anticipate similar stories circulating about Be Fair. I did not answer, I knew it was useless. People believe what they want to believe and if an attempt is made to dissuade them they are even more convinced that they are right.

Later that morning, Jack Le Goff and some of his United States 'squad' met me. They were genuinely sad; they had always held Be Fair in great esteem and told me that the taste of their victory was embittered by his misfortune, and they meant it. If he was unable to fly back to England with the others at the end of the week, they offered to look after him for me in America for as long as need be. Everyone I met, foreigners and patriots alike, seemed sad. Until Montreal I do not think I had appreciated the full extent to which Be Fair bewitched his admirers, but there he had so obviously been the crowd's favourite throughout and everyone seemed to have heard of him.

He stood uncomfortably in his stable. He had eaten and drunk a little and he had stopped kicking. He wanted peace that day and I did not spend much time with him. I could not maintain my composure if I looked at him for too long.

I mingled with the International showjumpers instead of my fellow eventers to watch the final phase of the Three Day Event. I did not expect many of them would know about Be Fair and therefore they would not look at me in that blank way. They all knew, but they were a great crowd and always ready to make anyone laugh.

The one other horse whose performance across country had compared with Be Fair's was a small, brown,

American thoroughbred mare, Ballycor. She won the gold medal for twenty-one-year-old Tad Coffin. Mike Plumb, as brilliant as ever on a comparative novice, won the silver and poor Shultz paid for Madrigal's abysmal lack of showjumping ability with two poles down and saw his gold fade into bronze. Richard Meade and Jacob Jones thoroughly deserved their fourth position as did the Americans their team gold.

The American team and, for obvious reasons, the British team were required at a press conference after the medal awarding ceremony had finished. I gained permission to fall out from Colonel Bill; I knew what sort of questions would be directed at me and I suspected that I might give them grounds for using the quote 'breaks down in tears at conference'.

I did not know what else to do then, so I went for a walk. I walked to the far end of the lake where the crowd did not pass as they trooped back to their cars.

Sitting on a boulder near the edge, I looked out across the water towards the stadium. A multitude of flags and gay colours filled the eye and on the right of the arena, rearing out of the steep bench-covered hillside, man-sized white lettering spelt out the word 'Bromont'.

Bromont.

Montreal. The 1976 Olympic Games – the culmination of a fairy-tale. But somewhere the cymbals had clashed too loudly and after seven years in Wonderland, Alice had woken up just a moment too soon. I looked down and saw a solitary feather near my feet. I stooped to pick it up. It was a soft, gentle colour, pale grey and brown – from a Canada Goose I imagined. I could not think what else to do so I counted the quills. Later that evening I left my boulder and returned to the stables. I gave the feather to Be Fair, leaving it protruding from one of his Good Luck telegrams pinned to his stable-door. The next morning it was gone.

Epilogue

Twelve months later his coat gleams a rich dark red. Beneath it his muscles are returning to their familiar proportions. He is a proud horse again.

We are alone in a hide-out far from home, thinking about each other, as I try to write his story. Alone together as we used to be during those first peaceful years, without the worry of other horses or the clamour of the outside world.

He is happy going out for rides in the country once again and thrilled if we find a fence to leap over; he was bored with the ten months he spent in the field.

People ask, 'Why are you getting him fit? What for?' I do not know what for. But I have no doubt that he will let me know his intentions; he has never found any difficulty in making them clear.

If it is hunting that he would like, then Tom Payne must have a day on him.

July 1977